Set Your
truth
free

A Twenty-Something's Guide to
Living a Truth- Filled Life

JASMINE PAUL

Set Your Truth Free:
A Twenty-Something's Guide to Living a Truth-Filled Life

Author: Jasmine Paul
Copyright © 2019 Find and Sustain LLC. All rights reserved.

Find and Sustain LLC
P.O. Box 320541
1002B S. Church Avenue
Tampa, FL 33679

ISBN: 978-1-7334538-1-3
eISBN: 978-1-7334538-0-6

Copyright © 2019 by Find and Sustain LLC.
Cover design by Erica Pebbles Fleras
Photo Credits by Malcolm Howe
Editing by Daphne Parsekian

This book was written out of love, pain, and confusion. Once I learned to speak my truth, I realized I wasn't alone. So many people have gone through similar situations, but they choose to keep it inside. Just like I did. Some mistakes and a few hardships later, I refuse to let things boil up inside of me. I refuse to sit back and watch my brothers and sisters around the world drown in silence. I set out to speak my truth daily and I hope you do the same.

– Jasmine Paul

Contents

Introduction

WHEN I STARTED WRITING this book, I aimed to offer young people a useful resource for college. Initially, this book contained scholarship information, college application guidance, counselor advice, and more. I delayed the publishing of this book for years. There are so many things I wrote then that are now obsolete or are readily available via the Internet or school resources. Instead, I compiled a collection of my thoughts and experiences that shaped my college and post-college years. I am writing to inspire, motivate, and challenge you to be the best YOU, you can be. I wish I could rewrite some parts of my journey, but maybe I went through those trials specifically to encourage someone like you!

My path is not the only way. There are millions of people who know better, have more experience, and have attained great success. My story doesn't exclude those who have come before or after me. I pray that my crooked path will encourage you to stay on yours. The Lord placed this book on my heart to share with the world. If it impacts just one person, I know he will be pleased! I truly believe someone will learn from my mistakes and it will prevent them from making their own. I'm writing to share my tests and trials, which have transformed into my testimony to the world. God brought me through and only he can take me to where I am headed.

I stalled the publishing of a book by six years. I chose to fill my time with other activities not relevant to the production of this book.

But, now it's time to re-focus on this book and God. This is His book. For you, it's time to get back to the vision the Lord placed in your heart as well. That vision didn't die; it's still there. It will grow and mature if you move out of the way.

My good friend Bre edited my first draft. (Thank you so much!) She believed this book was meant to touch the world. Young or old, those who are saved or people not sure about their spiritual journey should read this book. And guess what? We all deal with problems, and we all need someone or something to help us overcome the challenges we face. (Notice I said "help") The concept of this book is to assist and aid in setting your truth free. I will reflect on my most challenging situations throughout college and early adulthood like engaging with my weaknesses, smiling through failures, and crying during the hard times.

If you are looking for perfect answers with the perfect rules for life, you might want to close this book right now. If you are looking for a book about a person who has struggled, has shown anger toward God, has a strong work ethic that oftentimes looks a bit too much like perfectionism, admits to lazy seasons, cries and laughs so the world can hear and has learned many hard lessons along the way, keep reading. These are the lessons I wish someone had shared with me. I pray you learn these lessons and some more along the way. Some are meant to be followed, tweaked and/or broken. Ultimately, my prayer is that you learn to speak your truth. I pray you discover your identity and express who you are to the world for generations to come.

Are you ready to set your truth free? Maybe you're struggling to share your truth. Maybe you're in fear of losing out. Well, I'm here to share my truths with you. I want us to get up close and personal and I want you to be a little uncomfortable.

I believe we all should be transparent enough to share our truths. This book will walk you through the ins and outs of hiding from the truth, refusing to acknowledge the truth and the benefits of walking in your truth. I'll share some of the most intimidating and intimate parts of adulthood that you won't learn from school or maybe even your parents.

Truth #1 will focus on opportunities and how even the simplest tasks will lead to open doors. The second truth will focus on finances. I will walk you through my college debt process and how I paid it off entirely. I will show you how to maintain a budget and live more frugally to live your best life later. Truth #3 will highlight the importance of role models and mentors. I discuss the all-stars in my life and how you can find a mentor of your own. The fourth truth is tough. We get real close as I share my insecurities and flaws. Hopefully, through my sharing and exposure, it will enable you to face your insecurities and set them free. After uncovering insecurities, I will share how I healed. Self-care is vital to success and speaking your truth. I share how I take care of myself and how you can too in truth #5.

Once we learn about much-needed self-care, we will explore how to cultivate and protect the dreams God has given us. I will share how I spoke about my dreams to the wrong people and how you can disrupt dream killers who may try to suppress or kill your dream. After dreaming in truth #6, I will share how I manifested my dreams through various work experiences including internships and volunteer opportunities. Then we will talk about love and dating and uh... my current situation in truth #8. Truth #9 will share the importance of growing up and moving forward. After reading this book, the goal is for you to gain better insight for life after high school, college, a break-up, an illness or a plethora of life's difficulties and ease your transition into adulthood. Your journey won't be perfect, but you will experience lessons learned and tools to set your truth free.

After most chapters in this book, you will find a prayer. This prayer is for you to pray over yourself. Read the prayers and believe that God will do exactly what he said he was going to do. You alone have the power to speak truth over your life. For a long time, I didn't believe it. I relinquished so much power by believing everything but the truth. But those days are over. I'm speaking my truth whether people want to hear it or not. God gave me every experience in this book to grow closer to him but also to share it with someone like you. This is now our journey. Will you walk with me as we start setting our truth free?

Opportunity

How can I write a book? Will anyone even read it?

I DELAYED THE PUBLICATION OF this book for years because of doubt and fear. These doubts ushered in more questions, and then discouragement fueled my lack of motivation to finish. My delayed response to God's request meant countless missed opportunities.

Don't get me wrong; I don't think I can miss anything with God. I do think my delayed obedience, however, hindered my growth and the miracles this book would produce. I believe this opportunity needs to happen—now! I can no longer wait because the more I hold onto this book, the more opportunities I miss to write another book.

My passion for writing started at a young age. I published my first poem, "Tall," at the age of 7. It was a poem about my height (go figure!). I rhymed every word with "tall." My dad proudly hung my first published piece in our living room in Japan. "Tall" allowed me to speak freely. Writing began to shape my personality and allowed me to express myself. Writing became an escape for me.

My third-grade teacher, Ms. Mendel, cultivated my passion for writing. Ms. Mendel assigned weekly journal entries. Do you remember those black and white composition books with a cow-like print? I remember entering my weekly adventures in my journal. Our weekly assignments covered topics like school activities, homework, and family life. I decided to take it one step further and began to create short stories. These short stories were the incubators for my passion for the arts. They opened the door to share the release of my pain as I grew older. That release turned into freedom to pour out my soul through the spoken word. This freedom matured from short stories and poems to scripts and short films. My love for writing continued as I authored this book. All of these opportunities derived from my first poem, "Tall."

You may not understand the menial and trivial tasks that you are currently encountering. But those small lessons may be an opportunity in disguise. Don't discount your past, and don't lock away a desire God gave you. It may be years and years down the road, but fruition comes to those willing to be pruned.

What do I mean by pruning?

Go to John 15:1-17. This passage reflects abiding in Jesus, and through our obedience, we will reap the fruit. On the contrary, through our disobedience, we will not bear fruit or the fruit we bear may be rotten. Ew.

Imagine two apple trees: One is super green and lush and bears plenty of apples. The other tree is adjacent to the fruitful one, but it does not bear any apples. The branches are barely holding onto the trunk. The fruitful tree is receiving all the proper nutrients to thrive, while the other is not. I'm not saying to become an apple tree; I'm explaining that my season to flourish hadn't come yet. I wasn't ready to receive the blessings this book would produce; I wasn't ready to bear fruit, because I didn't desire to be pruned or disciplined.

Seven years later, I am finishing what I started (I mean what God started). I am declaring this opportunity in the name of Jesus. No matter how long it takes, do it! You see, it took me seven years, but I'm finally finished. Whatever season you're in, take the opportunities presented in front of you. Don't delay!

New Beginnings

Friend, you're probably in college, you have attended college, or maybe you are still figuring out what you want to do and haven't decided on a plan for your life. Too often we allow life to take us on journeys that we had no business in the first place. We choose certain paths, and God accompanies us along the way. Sometimes it's His will, and other times it is not. To me, "life" itself doesn't take us anywhere. The leading of the Holy Spirit guides us because we are afforded the grace to step out in faith and walk. I hope you can learn from my mistakes, make mistakes of your own, and create your path.

Life after high school is full of adventures and opportunities. New apprenticeships, shadowing college students, or starting a new job are welcoming into adulthood. It's a roller-coaster ride of ups and downs, lefts and rights, failing and succeeding. My best and worst decisions were made during my college career. There are decisions that I am still paying for today (some good and some bad).

The choice to seek higher education is not easy. If you've made that decision, good for you! But remember, college isn't for everyone.

Some of the greatest and most hardworking individuals in today's culture do not possess a college degree. So before you think that you're alone, you're not. Many people have never set foot in a classroom, but they have leaped ahead of their peers significantly in their respective fields.

If you're venturing to college, trade school, a new job, or an apprenticeship, it's time to go to work. It's time to make your own decisions and prepare for your future. I hope you can learn from my mistakes, make mistakes of your own, and create your path. You're also not alone Mistakes are driven by achieving goals, and achieving goals is driven by your definition of success. So what does success mean to you?

Defining Success

According to dictionary.com, "success" is defined as "the accomplishment of an aim or purpose, the good or bad outcome of an undertaking." Are you willing to accept the risk of failing? Failure is inevitable and it's a great feedback system on the ladder toward success.

Failure and I have a love-hate relationship. Failure restores my humanity and allows me to learn from my mistakes. On the contrary, my fear of failure is a huge reason why this book wasn't published sooner. I believed not finishing this book was better than the criticism I'd receive when it was published. I forgot that there is someone far greater than I am, and that's God. This is his book, and who am I to tell him what I am or am not going to do? After a slew of self-eliminating mantras and "I don't think I can do this," I decided to rely on him and shut off any negativity that I or anyone else created around me. I learned enjoy failing. Failing develops growth and maturity. I figure if I fail enough times, I'm bound to get it right eventually.

Achieve what is necessary to benefit your future success and happiness. Don't do it for anyone else but you! Imagine being rich with a wall in your home plastered with degrees, but you're completely miserable. What's the point? You've obtained great accomplishments at the expense of your happiness. Find whatever makes you excited to wake up every morning! Caution: This may take years to find, but that's okay. Success is a marathon, not a sprint. I changed my major three times in undergrad, I've changed my career field twice in the past six years, I've depleted my savings account and replenished it. Be flexible with change, and enjoy the life God has for you.

What Does Success Mean to You?

Success to me means having a loving and supportive family, obtaining my doctorate (as I write this, I have completed my first year, yay!), starting several businesses, and being a follower of Jesus Christ. My idea of success will differ from yours, and that's okay! Define success for yourself and remind yourself as often as you need to of this definition.

Are you a time watcher? Please stop now. Contrary to what many people believe, time is not being wasted. We can always be more effective and productive, but who hasn't wasted hours on social media? Life, especially adulthood, is a marathon, so enjoy it. Keep your eye on the prize. If it's meant to be, it will be.

Remember, the journey is not perfect! Your timeline will differ from mine or your friends. I didn't start applying to college until my senior year of high school. I submitted three college applications, and my first-choice school rejected me—Me, of all people? How could they do that? Didn't they know who I was? Or who I thought I was? I was crushed. The school I dreamed of attending did not give me access to their education. But God had a different plan in mind. I was accepted into my second-choice school, received a full-tuition scholarship, joined a sorority, interned at several companies, met my best friends (that are still my best friends today), graduated early, and received a commission in the United States Armed Forces. Everything aligned exactly how God wanted it to align. I continued to refine my truth even with failure and disappointment. I sought out every experience as an opportunity to grow and learn.

It's okay if your story ends differently than you planned. God takes us exactly where we need to go at just the right moment. Of course, sometimes it doesn't appear this way. In high school, I believed I was good enough to play college volleyball. I earned All-Conference titles and led my team to a seat in the state tournament. College scouts regularly recruited from my elite travel volleyball team. The majority of my travel volleyball team played college volleyball, except for me. I tried out for my college team and didn't make it. I was so heart-broken! I didn't get into my first-choice school and then didn't get a slot on the volleyball team. Interestingly enough, the same month of not making the team, I walked onto my school's Division 1 track and field team as a long jumper.

God allowed these failures to humble and groom me for the next stages of life. If I received everything I wanted, exactly the way I desired it, I would've never given God the glory. I would have believed that I received everything based on my merit, talent, and dedication.

An individual can work very hard, practice consistently, and still not achieve their desired outcome. The moment we release our lives into God's hands, something beautiful happens. God begins to take control and authorizes events and resources to merge and flow in our lives like never before.

As I write, I recall Psalm 91, specifically verse 5:

"You will not fear the terror of night, nor the arrows that fly by day." Why this verse? I had no idea what arrows were headed my way. I could've let those moments destroy me, but instead, I found a different course of action.

The unknown can be intimidating, but with God, you don't have anything to fear. I'm serious—anything! God takes us on an uneven, uncharted course, and if we allow ourselves to be open and flexible to the changes God has in store, we will find his peace that surpasses all understanding **(see Phil. 4:7)**. As you move on, I hope this section shows you to be mindful of the small, insignificant events of your life. Those moments can establish a routine or discipline that will last a lifetime.

A PRAYER FOR OPPORTUNITIES

God, I honor you today as Lord over my life. I pray that you will continue to grow and develop me. I pray your blessing over every opportunity that comes my way. I pray I will have discernment and obedience to know which opportunities to choose. I pray that I will use every day as an opportunity to draw near to you, to share my love of Christ, and to help someone get to know you. Thank you, Lord, for every opportunity. In Jesus' Name, Amen.

Finances

> *"Be content with what God has blessed you with. Trust God and don't lean on your understanding. He has given you every resource you need at this very moment."*

EVERYONE HATES AND LOVES the "F" word: finances. Why? Because it's pretty confusing. There's good and bad debt, real estate, stock portfolios, consolidation, art, collectibles, and so much more. For most people, going to college, unfortunately, means taking on debt. College tuition has increased exponentially: "The average tuition and fees at private national universities have jumped 157 percent. Out-of-state tuition and fees at public national universities have risen 194 percent, over the past twenty years."(Boyington[1], 2017) Eight years ago, I didn't think I would be debt-free. I took out a loan every year that I attended college. Once I graduated, I opted

---

1 Boyington, Briana. "See 20 Years of Tuition Growth at National Universities." U.S. News & World Report. Accessed July 19, 2017. https://www.usnews.com/education/best-colleges/paying-for-college/articles/2017-09-20/see-20-years-of-tuition-growth-at-national-universities

to defer payments because I started a graduate program and didn't believe I made enough money to pay them off. The more I deferred payments, the more interest I accrued. There was no end in sight, but I was determined to pay back the student loans as soon as possible. Seven years post-graduation, I am zero dollars in student loan debt.

You're probably wondering how I did it. Before we talk about my experience, let's outline this chapter. We'll discuss the following:

- Debt/student loans
- Constructing a budget
- Savings
- Future planning

These topics can be overwhelming for some. Sometimes they are even overwhelming for me. But hopefully, this information will introduce you to the financial planning of adulthood and will give you some insight into the future. It's not a "get rich quick" scheme or a "get out of debt free" card. I've provided a mixture of mistakes, choices, successes, and failures to highlight my financial journey. I am learning and relearning every day. Once I learn something, I share it to enlighten others. I believe we should all be successful mentally, physically, spiritually, emotionally, and financially. But what happens when you don't know how? I'll walk you through how I became financially unstable and how I learned how to transform my finances by trusting God.

What Got Me Here

Independence is my middle name. I'm 100% sure I received this trait from my mother. I've always wanted to work and earn my keep. At 14,

I DJed for a youth entertainment company, hosting birthday parties and other events (which probably sparked my love for entertainment). Unfortunately, I stopped booking consistent gigs, which led me to search for another job. After one year of babysitting and doing odd jobs for family members, I landed a grocery bagger position. It was simple; I strategically bagged the groceries and transported the well-packed bags to the customer's vehicle. I patiently waited for a tip. If it was my mom's groceries, I was almost guaranteed a $20 tip. (Thanks, Momma!) After ten months of bagging, I desired something more challenging and more income. I applied for a salaried position as a student store worker in the same store. This position offered a salary of $22,000 a year. For a 16-year-old, that's financial heaven. I worked there for two years until it was time for college.

I saved over $10,000 over two years. It did not take me long to learn the value of a dollar. Guess where the bulk of the money went? If you guessed clothes and shoes, you're partially correct (I know). The other portion went toward my degree that is proudly displayed on my mother's coffee table.

How did I save over $10K and still leave college with debt? The $10K was used for books and living expenses. I spent almost $5K in my first semester on books, clothes, emergency items, and food. After my first semester, I realized I was spending $1,200/month and I didn't have a job that could maintain my lifestyle. I made a more realistic $500/month budget. Looking back, I was living well above my means. My current Budget reflects $250/month for the same expenses. Remember how I mentioned being flexible with decisions? Adulting incorporates flexibility and navigating through circumstances, accepting risks, and making mistakes. Be okay with making mistakes. Adulthood is a new and unexplored territory for you. Be comfortable with adjusting and changing the way you look at money.

After graduation, I paid off close to one-third of my student loans. I successfully paid off $12,000 of my debt. YAY! I called the loan provider to figure out the rest of my debt. I found out that one of my loans, valued at $19,000, had grown to $25,000! Crazy! My eyes grew wide when the representative told me it would take 15 years to pay back the debt. Ummm...no! She didn't know me very well. I was not going to be in debt forever. No way!

I started writing this book in 2012 when I graduated from college. I commissioned and then began my active duty tour in the United States Armed Forces. My first assignment to CA encouraged me to have two roommates. Rent was expensive in California, but two roommates offset the costs. I aggressively saved 60% of my paycheck and consolidated my loans with a lower interest rate of 2.9%. I lived off of 40% of my paycheck during those first seven months of active duty. I direct deposited my checks to ensure that 60% went to savings. Bank fees (withdrawal charges from savings) reassured me that I would not touch my account. I never missed the 60% to savings because it was tucked away before I even realized it.

I saved over $12K, and I began aggressively paying down my loans. Dissolving chunks of my loans were like little victories for me. During tax season, the bulk of my return went to paying down the debt. A year later, I bought a house and quickly moved in a roommate. The roommate covered two-thirds of the mortgage, and I continued to pay down the loans with the extra money. I wrote for several blogs to add additional income to the debt. I *aggressively looked at debt as a matter of survival. It was either me or the debt, and I knew I was going to win. You should want to get out of debt by any means necessary! Honestly, if you can avoid debt, avoid it. I invested and saved at the same time, but my focus was on paying back my student loans.*

So what did my expenses look like in college? I started off having a modest budget but desired more material things as I got older. When you start adding all the miscellaneous expenses, the bills increase. Also, if you're spending about $1,200 a month on clothes and groceries, that will create more debt (at least in my case it did). Let's take a look at my college expenses during my freshman year of college.

First Semester College Expenses (estimates):

Items	Cost
Tuition and Fees	$22,500
Groceries	$1000
Textbooks	$300
Clothes	$1200
Spending Money	$2000
Total:	**$27,000**

As you can see from the chart, attending college was not cheap. In my first year, I spent over $27K. If spent wisely, that much money can buy you a new vehicle, a rental property (free and clear), an abundance of shares in the stock market, or a healthy down payment for a $200,000 home. Imagine, I was buying a rental property every year I went to college. If I had loans every year, I would have racked up over $100,000 in debt, not including interest. Fortunately, I had scholarships and grants that covered the difference. Scholarships allowed me to build meaningful relationships with financial coordinators, scholarship committees, and community leaders.

Relationships Matter

If you're in college, contact your school's financial aid department, and make them your friend. I'm serious. Be nice to them for two reasons:

1. You should be nice because they are human just like you (treat others how you want to be treated)
2. They hold the key to financial freedom and resources

A financial aid counselor can assist you with decisions that can impact your financial status as an adult. After graduating, I realized I made friends in every academic department. Why? Because connections make the world go around. You never know what connection can land you a job after graduation or who can write your recommendation letter to graduate school. Or, more importantly, who can call you when there's available money during the school year.

Scholarships

While sitting in the principal's office during my senior year, I overheard two parents discussing their child's scholarship. (I don't recall why I was there…but I digress.) My heart sank to my stomach because at that moment, I realized I hadn't begun planning for college. I desired to attend college, but I felt like I was behind the curve.

Being the super sleuth investigator that I was (and still am), I went home and stumbled upon a national and local scholarship database. Their website contained calendars to prioritize scholarships based on requirements and criteria (i.e., essays, transcripts, FAFSA, deadlines, etc.). That night, I researched numerous scholarships, and during the following weeks, I prepared college and scholarship applications. Do an Internet search for scholarships and grants in your local area. Many sororities and fraternities offer scholarships. Scholarships allow students to pay down their tuition and return to learning, which is the reason they entered college in the first place. After your tuition is paid, there may be excess funds available; some you should return, and other funds you should keep.

Refund Checks

If you earn numerous scholarships (and I encourage everyone to apply to as many scholarships as possible), the school will refund you the leftovers. For example, if you received $15,000 in outside scholarships (scholarships from local and national organizations), $3,000 in grant money (from the university), and $1,200 from the Pell Grant (from the federal government). Your tuition was only $15,000, so the school sends you a refund check of $4,200. That's right! Free money! The best part is, you don't have to pay it back. Amazing, right? I would use this money to invest, pay down debt, or pay it toward the next semester's costs.

Loans

A few years ago, I reviewed my loan activity and realized my last loan distribution was a refund check. This refund check was valued at over $5,000. What could I have possibly done with all that money? Back in 2010 (when I received this check), I shopped at several high-end clothing stores.

NOTE: These are the same stores I shop at today, but I make at least 10 times more now than I did as a student.

I recall spending Christmas break in London, twice. Bingo! I found where I spent one-third of the money, but I'm not sure where the other two-thirds disappeared to. My loan could've been much lower if I had returned the money to the loan provider.

Are you tracking? If I returned the money that was "refunded" to me, my loan would have been much less (about $5,000 plus interest less). Instead, I paid the loan provider for the loan, the refund check, and the interest charged on both. Nothing is wrong with the brands I chose to splurge on. However, now, from the perspective of a mature and financially fit adult, I don't think it was in my best interest as a struggling college student. I worked three jobs at one point. My priorities were not in the right place at the time.

My advice to anyone is to repay your refund checks, especially if they are from loans. If you are accumulating debt, pay the money back to your loan provider. It's hard to receive a $5,000 check and pay it back but fight the urge to spend it. You'll thank me later. Use part of the check for books, housing, or food. Try to save, save, save… and save some more. If you're knowledgeable about investing, put the refund check toward an investment.

In college, everyone knew when it was refund check time. Guys had brand new haircuts, new sneakers, and groceries in their fridge (sorry, fellas). Females had fresh manicures and pedicures, new outfits, and a girl's trip to Miami lined up. (I was one of you in my past life!) Refund checks are great, but if they are from loans, it's best that you pay them back, save them, or invest (depending on the rate and your knowledge/comfortability of investing—seek a financial advisor/counselor).

Do your research; I suggest following financial blogs, watching *YouTube* videos, and reading books on financial management. Scan the New York Times Bestsellers list and read them. There are great articles that share tips on savings, investments, debt management, and more. Please also read The Frugalista Files by Natalie McNeal. Natalie's experience was an eye-opener for my finances. Because of her, I incorporate a no-buy month into my financial year. Once you acquire the knowledge, don't hoard the information. Share it with those around you!

Making Cents

Friend, please take out a sheet of paper and write four realistic financial goals down. Let's do this together. When we are faced with reality, we will begin to brainstorm new ideas and resources to fund our goals.

Here were my financial goals for 2018:

- Save $21,000 in Emergency Savings by the end of 2018
- Max out retirement plan in 2018 ($18,500)
- Pay off car note by the end of 2018
- Payoff credit card debt balance monthly

You should have four realistic goals written down. I've been doing this for a while and continue to challenge myself with my goals. Place your written goals in a frame, and hang it where you have daily visibility. Writing down your goals keeps you accountable. Share these goals with a trusted individual who has experience in goal setting/financial planning. (Their life should be proof of this concept.)

Excuses, Excuses...

But, I don't make enough to save. This is a lie I told myself over and over. Save when you can, even if it's $10 a month. It's better than nothing. My income has increased four times over since 2012. However, I saved more money-making less than I do now. How can that be? In 2012 I had fewer responsibilities. At the time, I was paying rent and car insurance (no car notes thanks to Mom and Dad). I had little to no obligations other than cable, electricity, and water. Seven years later, my responsibilities have increased tremendously. I have another mouth to feed (my dog, Zeke) and other obligations, like tithes, leadership conferences, a mortgage, business expenses, and more. Save while you can! Don't be discouraged by the process. It gets better!

Budget Success

Planning and flexibility are two key factors for budget success. Planning is key to preparing budgets and flexibility is important when plans fail. Trust me, sometimes they do. Budgets take about six months to normalize. I recommend six months because if you've never budgeted before, you are essentially shocking your financial system. Imagine it's 90 degrees outside, and you arrive home to take a cool shower. Instead of setting the water on cool to ease your body into the temperature difference, you place it on cold. It's shocking, and you're probably going to perk up pretty quickly.

A budget is the same way. If this is your first time budgeting, you're shocking your thought process and mind to try something new. It's a good thing, but it takes time. Don't get frustrated when you overspend on groceries or gas. Implement a plan of attack to re-adjust your spending for the next month's budget. Continue this process until you get it right. I still struggle to regulate my budget; it's especially hard when you take a trip (that's not planned very well). Remember, preparation gives you flexibility when budgeting.

> " I share budgeting tips on my
> website: createfinstew.com"

Contentment

Please, don't live life like the Joneses. I repeat, don't live life like the Joneses! The fun stops when you're unable to pay your rent or purchase groceries. Live life based on your standards then reduce it by 10%. If you're saving toward your dream car, then save. If you desire to learn more about investing, then read investing books or connect with a trustworthy financial planner. Your neighbor or friend will always have something better than you (or what you think is better). Be content with all that God has given you. Trust God, and lean not on your understanding. He has given you every resource you need for this very moment.

Paul explains, "I am not saying this because I am in need, for I have learned to be content in whatever circumstances" **(Phil. 4:11).** Our circumstances change like the seasons. I remember being in seasons of abundance. I saved so much that I paid a portion of my car off with cash. I also recall seasons where I didn't have any money. I remember hearing the rumblings of my stomach, but I needed to pay rent instead. I remember when I learned how to have fun with my finances instead of building anxiety for fear of losing it all. The budget process is similar to your college, job search, and friend-making process. Do what's best for you. Be realistic in your circumstances, but ultimately, trust God. Even in my seasons where I thought I lacked, I didn't. In those seasons where I was "broke," I still never went without food or water. There was always a potluck or a college dinner I attended. The people who blessed me during this time were so gracious. God knew exactly how much I could handle and loved me.

Budgets Matter

Before establishing a budget, I never knew how I had less than $200 in my account before the next pay period. I retrieved the transaction history and saw that I had depleted my account. Reader, this is what it looks like when you opt to live paycheck to paycheck. You begin to exhaust one paycheck and itch for the next one.

After a few years of living like this, I decided to take charge of my finances and improve my financial situation. I started budgeting and rapidly paying off debt. Currently, I have two home mortgages.

I pay off my credit card as soon as I create a balance so I don't pay interest. Now I tell my money exactly where to go. It wasn't always like this. I'd racked up over $10K in credit card debt at one point. I've made mistakes with finances and will continue to make them. My goal is to learn from my mistakes, share how I overcome, and show you that you will learn to adapt to different situations. I challenge you to go outside of your comfort zone and take control of your finances—now. My creative financial stewardship course designs finances for people like you and me—people who aren't sure where to go but don't want to leave it at "Well, it will all work out." We keep it simple and give God the room and space to bless us.

Closed Mouths Don't Eat

If you need help, ask for it. I suggest talking with a financial counselor, contacting your bank (most banks offer free financial advising), or seeking out a mentor (anyone who knows a thing or two about finances). Be real and honest. For some reason, people choose to keep their finances a secret, but the majority of young people struggle with understanding finances. My friends and I discuss finances all the time. As a result, we have paid off loans, purchased homes, and expanded our investment portfolios.

Your friends should become your accountability partners. Instead of watching the newest summer flick, stay in and enjoy a rented movie or go on a day when the movie theater prices are reduced. Plan a vision board party to organize goals for the next year. A few years ago, my best friend came to visit me in my new home. I had zero furniture, but I had blankets. We crashed on the floor and watched movies all day under blankets. True friends will love you, respect your financial goals, and get comfortable on your blankets!

While in college, I worked three jobs, and my income could never afford the finer things in life. The time spent with my friends, however, was invaluable. Even now, when one of my best friends visits, we end up in the kitchen cooking and laughing. We cherish our time with one another. We are aware of our financial goals, and we partake in activities that are low-cost or free, like attending the National Museum of African-American History and Culture in D.C. (two times in one weekend) or heading to Essence Music Festival in New Orleans. Our salaries have doubled, but we still maintain a healthy, financially sustaining, and wealth-growing lifestyle. We actively communicate our goals to ensure we maintain this lifestyle.

We speak our truth with one another even if it hurts to share. We're open and honest, which allows us to grow and mature.

The next few paragraphs are habits I've learned and developed along the way. They are lessons that I maintain to this day. Hopefully, these lessons are something you already know or something you can glean.

Find good friends. Pray for them. True friends can be enablers and encouragers when it comes to finances. My friends keep me accountable, and they ensure I'm staying consistent with my budget. Host a sushi-making party instead of eating out at the popular Japanese restaurant. Plan a potluck for the ingredients. Your crew is saving money because everyone is pitching in, and you're also having a great time together.

Life Lessons

Pay yourself first. Even if you aren't bringing home your ideal paycheck yet, set aside $10–$50 each month toward an emergency fund. If an emergency occurs, you're more equipped to handle life's surprises. Remember, this emergency fund is not for an impromptu shoe sale or a coffee run. Save this money for an emergency (like when your tires need to be replaced or your car battery dies— both have happened to me unexpectedly).

Swap meet with your friends. Most of my home décor is from my friends' garages or basements. You'd be surprised how many untouched gems are sitting in your friends' living spaces. This swap is not limited to housewares; it can be unused/used hair products, gently worn clothing, food spices, furniture, and more! (My best friend gave me her Serta mattress because my mattress was, uhh, broken—book coming soon about this.) If you have something you don't need, don't throw it away; trade it or donate it. One day, after organizing my closet, I donated my unwanted clothes to Goodwill. The next week while shopping, my friend picked up a jacket I donated. She turned to me and asked, "Why didn't you just give it to me?" I didn't even think about it. Now, I wouldn't go to the extreme and start sharing underwear or toothbrushes (that's not healthy), but someone's unused clutter can be another person's treasure.

Prepare your meals. You can save a significant amount of money if you cook your food. Did your parents or teachers warn you about the freshman 30? Well, it's true. You can gain up to 30 pounds of weight during your freshman year due to a lack of exercise and poor eating habits. Take advantage of your meal plan (you already paid for it), and go to the salad bar instead of the pizza line. Remember, what you consume determines how much energy and effort you can put into your studies.

I limit my meat intake and avoid fried foods. Eating healthy is inexpensive. I don't buy meat products, and most of my fruits and vegetables are locally grown. My grocery bill ranges from $50 to $80 every two weeks. It wasn't always like this though. I used to frequent the pizza bar during my freshman year.

If you live off-campus, prepare your food, if you can. I know it takes time and energy, but it is cost-effective. Research recipes online, or pick up a cookbook. Use meal-prepping apps like *MealLime* to cut down on grocery store time. Here's a list of ingredients for a simple chicken breast dinner (about 5–6 servings):

Sample Meal Preparation List

Items	Cost
Chicken Breast	$7.00
Rice	$3.00
Spinach	$3.50
Broccoli	$5.00
Total	**$18.50**

If you cook five servings, you're paying $3.70 per meal; if you stretch it to six servings, it's $3.10 per meal. Since you're the preparer, you choose whether to add salt, sugar, oil, etc. I enjoy eating out, but because I'm so picky, I'd rather cook my food and save money.

The best prices for your textbooks aren't found in your school's bookstore. Stop paying full price for textbooks! I strongly encourage you to rent/buy your textbooks from online websites. I spent less than $850 on books during my three and a half years of college. Some professors author books, so you may have to suck it up and pay full price. Think of it as supporting a local business. If you're sitting in a class that's not your major, exclusively rent books. (Unless you like the book, then, by all means, buy it.) Hopefully, this chapter provided you with more insight to better financially plan. Tell me if you've learned something from this chapter at info@createfinstew.com.

Application:

- Check your credit report annually on www.annualcreditreport. com
- Follow finance bloggers who give free tips on saving and investing.
- Pray over your finances and trust God!
- Read books that offer wealth-building advice. *(Check out my list at the end of this book.)*

A PRAYER FOR FINANCES

Most Gracious Father, I humbly kneel at your feet today. I pray that my financial journey will be impacted in a positive way. I pray that I will release anxiety about my debt or financial behavior and sharpen my tools with financial wisdom. I pray that I will be surrounded by friends and family who will encourage me on my financial journey. I pray my decisions will be a blessing and not a hindrance. I pray I will learn to be the lender and not the borrower. I pray that you will do exceedingly and abundantly above all that I can ask or think! I pray your blessings into my life right now. I pray that I will cling to you and know that you are my provider! I can and will do ALL things through Christ who strengthens me! In Your Precious Son's Name, Amen.

Role Models And Mentors

"Listen to their advice, but ensure that you make the final decision for your development and peace."

A FEW YEARS AGO, I attended a conference, and the keynote speaker asked the audience, "Aside from your parents, siblings, significant others, and best friends, who can you call at 3 a.m.? If you can name two people, consider them your mentors." Can you name two people right now that you can call in the middle of the night? If you can, then you're ahead of the game. If not, pay attention.

Mentors are like the parents you never had. Mentors are young and old, male and female, personal and professional, and everything in between. Mentors are a unique group that provides sound counsel and wisdom. I lean heavily on my mentors; they assist me spiritually, emotionally, professionally, and personally.

Older, Younger...? Does It Matter?

As a young person, I've always gravitated toward more mature and wise individuals. (This is probably why I am slightly awkward around my peers.) I strive to learn as much as I can from those who came before me. Mentors share stories of trials, tribulations, successes, and failures. My mentors have so much wisdom, and whether I like it or not, most of them have been where I've been and have gone where I'm going. A good mentor is someone who picks up the phone and asks, "How are you doing?" This is usually done on a quarterly or monthly basis. (In my case, they call because I haven't updated them on my life, and they are wondering where the heck I've been!)

Mentors possess quality listening skills. This unique bunch cares about your future, and they are invested in your growth and development. Listening to you is a vital part of understanding your problems and connecting with you as a person. These mentors may not understand the new slang or the latest app, but they possess valuable knowledge that transcends generations. Listening is key because mentors shouldn't force you to come to a decision; instead, they present options to better mold your decision.

Mentors celebrate successes and provide comfort during failures. Because they don't hold the same biases as friends or parents, they have the opportunity, to be honest, and raw. They have different experiences and want the best for you. My mentors never sugarcoat anything with me, and I wouldn't have it any other way. The truth is never easy to hear. "Then you will know the truth and the truth shall set you free," God speaks truth to his children. He is not a God who lies, and quite frankly, why would he? So your mentors shouldn't lie either.

"God desires His people to seek the truth and think about those things. When mentoring, seek counsel from individuals who will reveal the truth to you.

Phil 4:18 "Finally, brothers and sisters, whatever is true,
whatever is noble, whatever is right, whatever is pure,
whatever is lovely, whatever is admirable—if anything
is excellent or praiseworthy—think about such things'"

I am more likely to respond in a situation to someone who is not a friend or family member. Why? Mentors have nothing to lose. I listen carefully and intently when my mentors speak because I respect them and know they have my best interests at heart. This is not a rebellion against my parents or friends. I truly love them, but I am stubborn. I need positive reinforcement that is better received from my mentors.

Good and Bad Mentors

There are good mentors and there are bad mentors. Not all people were meant to lead or mentor. Mentors should take their mentee to places they've been or should at least be able to guide the way. Life cycles through seasons. There are seasons of planting, growth, drought, and harvest. There may be mentors that outgrow you and some you outgrow. Sometimes you have to cycle people in and out of your life, just like friends and relationships (not if you're married or have children—there's no cycling there). Your mentors stimulate and shape your growth on the path of success.

The relationship between mentor and mentee is given and taken. They check in on me, but I check in on them as well. I celebrate their successes and admire their perseverance in life. Their feats and accomplishments inspire me to keep going. Their pride and celebration remind me of where I've been and where I'm headed. My mentors keep me sane and motivated, and they promote balance in my somewhat unstable life. Choosing a mentor is key in developing the future plans of your career and your life.

Chemistry

How did I obtain my mentors? Well, I never stopped calling. Traditionally, I am reserved, and it takes a bit of an effort to get me to open up. When someone genuinely gets to know me, I interpret that effort as relationship building. My mentors strategically entered into my life, and I accepted it. Fortunately, I'm not shy, so talking to people older than me didn't matter. They push me more than I could push myself. They have experience and wisdom that I currently don't possess.

How do you make friends? Usually, there's something attractive about the person that draws you to them. It could be their laughter, personality, or motivation that pulls you closer to this person. After a few lunches/dinners and phone conversations, you are both interested in pursuing a friendship. The friendship grows as you move past coffee dates to sleepovers. This person comforts you during times of sorrow or is the shoulder you lean on when heartbreak occurs. You value this relationship and make friendship a priority. Establishing friendships is easy, and so are mentor relationships. The mentor or mentee has attracted the other, and over time, a relationship is formed.

I can't exactly describe it, but you just know. Your potential mentor will be comfortable around you and vice versa. They will check in on you, and it won't seem as if they are pushy or nosy. They genuinely care about your well-being and interests. My mentors have written recommendation letters for scholarships, referred me to jobs, and assisted in securing an apartment for me. They're more than professional resources too. I seek love and spiritual advice from several of my mentors. I admire their relationships with their spouses and hope to experience love like that one day. They share examples from their marriages with me on my journey. Mentors will let you know when you're dealing with a scrub. (I have had my heart saved from heartbreak numerous times.)

Establishing relationships with these trusted few will pave the way for more connections and a better understanding of your industry and career field as well as promote comfortability with yourself and your future. Listen to their advice, but ensure you make the final decision for your development and peace.

Advising

College advisors, like mentors, offer great advice too. I've heard horror stories about college advisors that have signed students up for the wrong classes, which delayed their graduation. Many might blame the advisor, but I partially blame the student. Each university has a curriculum that is published for the school year. Upon choosing a major, a student receives the curriculum. (It can be viewed online as well.) The student should register for classes based on the availability of the class, their available time, and the curriculum. Becoming a grown-up requires discipline and attentiveness. You hold the keys to your future and you should never relinquish that power to someone else.

Be active and engaged in your future. Know your advisor's name, office hours, email address, and office location. This is one relationship that needs to be solid and important to you. An advisor can make or break your college career.

I can only attest to my own experiences with my advisor, but I had his email address, office number, and office hours on my phone.

I wanted to graduate early, so it was imperative for me to constantly check the curriculum and communicate with him to game plan my college career. (Notice how I provided him with a game plan, it's the same concept with mentors. Advisors are intended to advise, not decide.) You hold the keys to your future, and you should never relinquish that power to someone else.

Fortunately, I participated in ROTC, which required cadets to track their college careers on a spreadsheet. This form enabled us to map out our entire college course schedule from freshman year to senior year. I recorded my class names and credit hours earned. I suggest you create a similar chart mapping out your courses, credit hours, dates accomplished, and a running total for your credit hours. Update this chart throughout the semester, and share it with advisors to make sure you're on track.

A Daily Interview

First impressions are lasting impressions. Here's what I don't want you to do: sit in the back row on the first day of class and remain there. College is practice before stepping into the real world! If you sit back in your classes, you may harbor the habit to sit back in the boardroom or a staff meeting. If you don't learn to speak up and engage now, it may be a slow transition into the workplace, the home front, or whatever your situation is after high school. My boss reminds me that I'm on a daily interview. Just because I am in the seat now doesn't mean I'll remain there.

Every relationship you form as an adult is a daily interview. We must constantly make an effort to grow and stretch the relationship or it becomes stagnant. I know it might sound challenging, but you do this every day, whether it's with friends or teammates. You are being interviewed daily, and you should do the same for others in your life.

To this day, I email my teachers three weeks before beginning class. I establish a rapport with them and show my enthusiasm for the class. I don't suck up, but I take advantage of getting to know a teacher outside the classroom. Because I learned how to communicate with teachers, I am comfortable communicating with supervisors and senior leaders in my organization. I reach out to future co-workers and supervisors to introduce myself and share with them my excitement for the new job. See the transition from college to work-life?

In college, I visited my teachers randomly throughout the day. My visits became so frequent that my teachers wondered if something was wrong with me if I didn't visit them. I became a sponge and absorbed as much as I could from them.

I studied media production in college and my instructors were involved in other projects, including films, dissertations, and speaking engagements, that caught my interest. I connected with my instructors outside of the classroom, which developed me professionally and personally.

I engaged in conversations about the arts, politics, and more. Professors also make great mentors. Become the face behind your name, and get to know your teachers. You'll be surprised by their interests, insights, and willingness to get to know you and help you. College offers a unique opportunity to impress not only your teachers but your peers. Remember, your peers are important too, but I will touch on that later.

Career Services

Career services are located on virtually every campus throughout the United States. These centers offer resume help, interview preparation, a resource of influential alumni, and a database of jobs, internships, and more. These services were offered for free at my school. Check to see what your school offers.

The career advisors helped me highlight my key experiences and discard any unnecessary information not relevant for a resume. Observe them while they are updating your resume. This resource won't last forever, and you'll need to know how to update it when you graduate. Free career services are oftentimes available up to six months after graduation. Colleges know the difficulty of obtaining a job right after graduation. After determining your class schedule and weekly routine, locate your campus's career services department and schedule an appointment.

"My favorite career counselor, Eric Melniczek, ran the Career Services Department at High Point University. He has helped many students land their dream jobs and internships. I credit many of my successes to Eric's diligence and patience to his work and students. He motivated me to obtain every opportunity that came my way. (Thank you, Eric!) Every few months, I attended one of his career services classes. While in the career center, I updated my résumé or attended an interview workshop."

Networking Across

Issa Rae, author of The Misadventures of Awkward Black Girl and the director of the HBO series, Insecure, stated in an interview with NewsOne, "Network across, see who's struggling, see who's in the trenches with you." Her interview made me revisit the purpose of this book and the purpose of my life. I enjoy creating and curating with more mature and experienced adults. I struggled with relating to my peers, especially while in high school and college. I impressed my professors, but people my age came with challenges. It was hard to network across. At one point, I thought I didn't need them. I thought I could survive without them, which resulted in burned bridges. I realized as a more mature adult that this is not true at all! I need my peers more than ever. These men and women are my support systems and accountability partners.

Collaboration is key. This book was shared among my friends' circle. I trusted them and knew that they would be the first people to encourage and criticize me. Do I expect them to buy a copy? Not really, but I know they are supportive, no matter what. You'll see later that I asked some all-stars to share their stories in this book. Why? Because I respect and value their opinions. They are working just as hard as I am, probably even harder, to build their empire. I solicited their truth and experience because I know it's value-added. You need to hear their stories and the stories of others working alongside you. I believe it's important for everyone's story to be heard. It can inspire and encourage someone to do better or to keep going. Stay connected, and be great!

Application:

- Family members make great mentors.
- Mentors come in different varieties and capacities.
- Be active in the mentee–mentor relationship.
- Utilize mentors in all areas of your life, professionally and personally.
- Mentorship is a two-way street, regardless if you're the mentee or the mentor.
- Keep in touch. Try to engage with mentors every two to three months.
- Local non-profit organizations and Chamber of Commerces offer career counseling and sometimes free classes.

A PRAYER FOR ROLE MODELS AND MENTORS

Lord, thank you for this day and for the grace to live my life for one more day. Today, I pray you will bring mentors and role models into my life who will pour into me. I pray, Lord, that you will cultivate our relationship. I pray, God, that in our season of mentorship, we will both grow and develop as better people. As Moses mentored Joshua and Samuel mentored David, I pray you will send me a God-fearing woman or man of God to groom me to be the person you desire me to be. Thank you, Lord. Amen.

Insecure Much...

"Maybe, every time we have a sliver of doubt, we should replace 'I' with 'God' and see how silly we sound."

M Y CURRENT FAVORITE TELEVISION show is *Insecure*. This show follows young people of color striving to overcome their insecurities. I see so much of myself in the show. Why? Because I can be insecure. I'm insecure about my looks, my relationships, my career, and even my faith at times. Don't get me wrong; I'm a confident woman. I hold my head up pretty high; I love my natural hair and less than rigid nose. When I like a guy, I become head over heels and tend to love hard (if they let me). I love my career, but I can be insecure about the projects I create. And my faith...well, when I sin or fall short, I judge myself as if I'm God.

Instead of going to God in repentance, I attempt to become God, and it never works. I have issues, and I'm sure you have some too—and that's okay. We're all somewhat insecure, but the decision to stay insecure or overcome our insecurities must be made. We have the power to conquer these little inadequacies that we place on ourselves.

This chapter will expose the things that make us question ourselves and how we can overcome them. We may struggle with relationships; however, we must fully surrender those areas of weakness to Christ. I'm hoping that this chapter will help you uncover your insecurities and you learn to be secure in your truth.

"We have the power to conquer these little
inadequacies that we think of our self."

Am I Qualified?

Too many times I hear people spread lies about themselves to include but not limited to: "I'm not qualified. I'm not good enough. I don't have enough money. I need more time." I can't lie; I've even had this untrue form of thinking too. This mindset not only hinders our dreams but it's a slap in the face to God. God can do all things, so if we believe that we cannot do it, we are telling God, "God, I know you're mighty and powerful, but what you're doing is not good enough." Maybe, every time we have a sliver of doubt, we should replace "I" with "God" and see how silly we sound. Let's try it: "I cannot write this book." Now replace it with "God cannot write this book." See, it doesn't even make sense.

I believe we have to reverse our thought patterns and get back to the basics. Don't count yourself out! When you recognize a road-block ahead of you, don't stop. Slow down, observe the situation, and give it to God. In all honesty, my best moments in life were when a "roadblock" tried to stop my progress. It didn't derail my journey but instead made it greater. I diminished that block to a small pebble and kept pushing. Don't get me wrong. At the moment, I felt like I couldn't continue. When these moments creep up, I remind myself of God's promises in His Word:

Psalm 23:1 "The Lord is my shepherd, I lack nothing."

Psalms 103:8 "The Lord is compassionate and gracious, slow to anger, abounding in love."

Jeremiah 20:11 "The Lord is with me like a mighty warrior."

Hosea 10:12 "...it is time to seek the Lord until He comes and showers His righteousness on you."

War

As an Armed Forces member, I am required to be fit to fight. I must be in shape (physically, mentally, and emotionally) because I can deploy at any time. During deployment, a soldier could be exposed to hostile actions. To protect from potential hostile events, body armor is required when exposed to high threat levels. The armor is fitted to equip and protect the soldier.

In addition to the armor, the soldier must have ammunition, a lighting flare, a medical kit, etc. The soldier must be prepared for imminent danger at all times. The time to locate the position of the medical kit is not when the soldier or his teammate is injured. The kit must be studied to ensure it is just right for the soldier's use.

The Bible is no different. Although we have the opportunity to open it up, the time to find a scripture is not in the presence of the enemy. It's when you're in the safe zone and you have an opportunity to draw near to God. In case of a spiritual attack, a Bible may not be readily accessible, but the scriptures buried deep in your heart can serve as ammunition. Of course, life doesn't always work out like this. You may be in the middle of an attack and I recommend grabbing the closest Bible or recalling a scripture you know. Are you ready for war, or do you need to study and practice before war breaks out? What does war look like when you're not even sure you're in a battle?

"Are you ready for war or do you need to study and practice before war breaks out?"

"Don't Be Afraid of Your Tears"

I have reservations about sharing my weaknesses with others, but I didn't know the power of people or collaboration until I was in my moment of weakness. My vulnerability allowed another person the opportunity to help me. It makes so much sense, right? When you ask for help, people will listen. After years of hiding my vulnerabilities, I try to be as transparent as possible. It's not to put my business out there but to be honest with myself and those around me.

One day, I had tea (I don't drink coffee) date with an amazing woman. Her statement would change my life forever: "Don't be afraid of your tears." Wow! It was so simple yet powerful. As she spoke those words to me, tears immediately rushed down my face. Before this moment, I had allowed anxiety and fear to disrupt my peace. Throughout this season, I cried, but I didn't know why I was crying.

Over tea, I uncovered what I was feeling stemmed from fear. I was afraid to face reality. I was afraid to face the fact that I actually might die and leave behind my family and friends. I won't go into much detail because I am writing another book about it, but this woman's heart touched mine that day. Because of her transparency and faith, I was able to conquer my fears.

Our tears bring healing power. Have you had a really good cry lately? The kind where you have snot all over your face and you don't even care? You rise from the sea of tears refreshed. The flowing tears are an outward expression of an internal reflection. Your tears will empower and challenge you, but you can't stop at the tears. Tears require action.

Have you ever cut into an onion? What happens after you cut into it? About one to two chops in, tears start running down your face, and your eyes burn. (I purposely buy chopped onions for this very reason.) Onions produce the chemical irritant known as syn-pro-pane- thial-S-oxide. It stimulates the eyes' lachrymal glands so they release tears. An external situation (cutting onions) is causing a physical reaction (tears)[2].

An intense situation causes an emotional reaction. These situations could range from being rejected from your dream school to getting fired from a job, not having enough money for rent, or breaking up with a guy you thought you were supposed to marry. (All have happened to me.) But now that you've cried about it, what are you going to do next? Will you sit and cry for months and months, or will you seek counsel?

I encourage you to ask for help when you need it and accept the help when you receive it. We can't do this life on Earth by ourselves. We need people—people who will pick us up, people who are willing to share their homes and food—and people need people just like you.

---

2   Why does chopping an onion make you cry?" Library of Congress Web Site. Accessed October 7, 2017. https://www.loc.gov/rr/scitech/mysteries/onion.html.

Help!

Sometimes it's hard to ask for help, especially when we think we have it all together. Help is your best friend. Don't be afraid to ask for help, and learn to embrace what you receive. Allow yourself to be open to accepting that you don't know everything. Those that ask for help and accept it do better in life than those who sit around doing nothing (my opinion, of course).

Freshman year, I took Pre-Calculus 101, and I was nervous. I was halfway through the semester and received a C- on my mid-term. I couldn't accept a C for a grade, so my professor suggested tutoring. There I was on the bottom floor of my school's library asking myself, Do I need this? Maybe, I can get by... After arguing with myself, I realized, Yes, I need this!

My tutor, Mary, and I met every other day for two hours. She helped me understand my calculator (a TI something—I have no idea how to use it now), comprehend formulas, and complete my homework. She tested my knowledge with weekly quizzes.

At the end of the semester, I received a 98% in the class, which exempted me from taking the final exam. I was so proud that my hard work paid off. I struggled, but the help I received enabled me to do better than when I started. This habit of asking for help formed slowly, but I continue to ask for help today on the job, in ministry with schoolwork, and with relationships. There are smarter people in the world than me, and I trust their experiences. I am okay with not knowing everything, and I trust others will lead and guide me.

"Don't be afraid to ask for help and learn
to embrace what you receive."

Free Help

Schools offer tutoring programs (usually free), disability accom-
modations, writing labs, and more for their students. As a student,
you must be willing to seek these services and receive the help you
need. Don't be discouraged by not understanding the material. Be
bold enough to say you need help! This ability to ask for help will
maintain throughout your life. I needed assistance for buying a
home, entering a doctorate program, and becoming a wife (not one
yet, but he's coming).

Seek friends for help as well. I can't tell you the number of times
that my sorority sisters and colleagues proofread my papers and
assignments. Remember my friend Bre? She did the first edit of this
book. She's one of the reasons why this book is finally being published.
While in graduate school, I had close friends review my work. When
you're writing a ten-page paper or a book, the last thing you need
is mistakes. If they're true friends, they'll read over your work (just
give them enough time). My best friend, Lauren, also proofread my
papers for my doctoral program. Although pride creeps in (because
she's a tough critic), I know she has my best interest at heart.

Help is a two-way street. The same way you reach out to your
friends for help, your friends should be able to do the same with you.
Can I be real with you? I can't express enough how important it is
to ask for help. I wish I understood this concept sooner. I entered
my senior year of college and didn't have housing. My sorority sister
and I were going to be roommates, but because of pride, I detached
from the relationship and opted not to live with her. (We are good
friends now. It was petty girl stuff.) At the last second, I secured an
apartment and lived by myself. My income didn't fully cover the
expenses at the apartment. I broke the lease and lived out of my car

for the next two months. Talk about instability! I bounced between two living situations: my friend's couch and my friend's floor. The only people who knew about my homelessness were the friends who let me crash. I never mentioned it to my parents or my sorority sisters. Why? Because of pride.

I was afraid of the image I'd portray. I was so "tough" and "resilient" that I didn't realize I was hurting myself in the process. Resilience and toughness have nothing to do with pride. Pride is a weakness, in my opinion. When you are capable of being real with yourself and your situation, that is strength. I learned, especially through ministry, that I have to be transparent. God requires it. The people you serve require it. He doesn't want the cleaned-up version of me. He wants my brokenness and pain so that he can rework it into his masterpiece. When I am weak, he is strong.

During my homelessness, my grades slipped. I ate out all the time. I wasn't focused. I slept in my car some nights. I wished I had help, but I didn't know how to ask for it. My friends and parents would have helped if they only knew. Unfortunately, because of my lack of communication, I put myself in danger. When I hit rock bottom, my friend offered to let me stay at her place full-time! Rent was $200 a month, and I had my bedroom and bathroom. I finally had my place and a room to myself.

I should have approached the situation like I did my math class. Failure was not an option, yet in this situation, I failed. This situation occurred three years after I received tutoring. I needed to learn this lesson again because when faced with the impossible, I chose not to ask for help. Remember, we are human and make mistakes. We're not weak because we ask for help. We show our strength through weakness.

Be Gentle with Yourself

In the past, I bottled up my emotions and hold them in until I exploded. It usually didn't end well, and my relationships and projects suffered. I allowed the emotions to fester, which enabled me to create alternate scenarios in my head. 'This happened to me because I didn't go to the store on time. If I had only reached out to him sooner, this wouldn't have happened.' God knows exactly what he is doing, and I don't have to be him to decide what I deserve. My response should be yes without hesitation or reservation. I am my own worst enemy, and maybe you are yours too.

I'm conscious to purge my mind of ill-thinking. Negativity can slow your progression with school, work, relationships, and life. Vent as often as you can to people you trust. Everyone deserves a moment to release (some more than others). Grab a trusted individual who will listen, and let it all out. Life is demanding at times and it's unhealthy to keep it bottled inside. Mental health is important, too. It's fragile and should be exercised frequently, like healthy eating and working out. I recommend finding a counselor or psychologist, not just for the hard times but for the good times as well. Counselors offer a unique perspective and can help you cope with a loss or form better communication skills with family and friends.

Whatever the situation, it's time to conquer the challenges of life. Producing kind thoughts leads to positive actions. Be gentle with yourself. The world can treat us poorly, so we have no business adding to it. Fear and anxiety promote inactivity, stunted growth, and a deplorable demeanor. Who wants to be around someone like that? What you think and believe will eventually come to fruition. Be careful and intentional about letting go of fear and trusting in God and yourself.

Attitude, New Heights

Ever hear the phrase "Your attitude determines your altitude"? I hate to be cliché, but it's true. I'd rather study or work with someone who is a "Positive Patty" than a "Negative Nancy." Someone who sees the positivity in any situation will more than likely excel and go much further than someone who doesn't.

The opportunity to change your attitude to a positive one will always reap rewards. You will see doors open that you once saw closed. You don't have to smile from ear to ear each day (I do because I choose to), but I encourage you to look at your situation as an opportunity. Focus on the positive aspects of the situation. If you want to smile, then smile away! You never know the internal battles someone else is facing, and your positive attitude could potentially enable them to make a change in their life for the better.

Overcoming the Past

Growing up, I was tainted by the world's opinion of me. I attended a private, predominantly Caucasian, Catholic middle school. I was the token African-American student in my grade. My friends had bright blue and green eyes and long blond and brunette hair. I had medium-length, relaxed hair that I wore in intricate braided styles created by my salon-owner aunt. I always questioned, "Why aren't I lighter? Why doesn't my hair flow like my friends'? Why is my nose so big?" These were a few hateful questions, among others, that I asked myself.

My mom's friends encouraged me and informed me of my beauty, but it meant nothing to me. I didn't think I was beautiful compared to my porcelain buddies. I was a dark-skinned girl with Caribbean features. Surely I wasn't beautiful. There weren't many people in the media who looked like me either, and it made me question my beauty. My mom was beautiful, but I didn't feel like I resembled her. I inherited almond-shaped eyes, semi-coily hair, and brown, mocha-tinted skin. My eyes were brown, and my nose had little to no definition. The lack of architectural structure in my nose allowed my glasses to slide down constantly.

They always slid down, and I would push them up, just for them to slide down my nose minutes later. (I now realize that I need to tighten the ends of the glasses around my ears to hold them up, thank God!) I continued to compare myself to others in high school. I attended a public high school and finally had friends who looked like me. It wasn't until my senior year of high school that I started to appreciate myself for who I was: the woman God created me to be.

I entered college with a whole new attitude—a little too much attitude if you ask me. I was sure of myself and confident. My style evolved into an outspoken, Afro-centric, urban, loud, attitude-filled, success-oriented rock star. This newfound self-awareness allowed me to define my truth. I was finally able to be myself. I was able to be unapologetically me.

It wasn't until I moved away from home and lived on my own that I could explore and be who I was. I balanced my work schedule and homework assignments, attended or didn't attend parties (most likely attended), shopped for groceries and clothes, created the circle of friends I wanted, and more. I was the provider now; I made the choices that impacted my life. It wasn't until college that I began exploring me.

Maybe you're still figuring out who you are, or maybe you know exactly who you are and no one can tell you otherwise. Either way, I pray you strive to be the best version of yourself daily. Insecurities are challenging and they eat away at the best version of you. We have the power to overcome them and to help others struggling as well. Pray this prayer consistently; tell yourself you are beautiful and smart because you are! Surround yourself with men and women who believe the same! You can and will overcome.

A PRAYER FOR INSECURITIES

God, I thank you for me. I thank you for creating me with all my flaws and quirks. I thank you for allowing me to be me in all of my mess (well, what I think is a mess). You love me beyond all reproach. You have fearfully and wonderfully made me, and I rejoice over that truth. God, today I lay my burdens at your altar; I lay all my complexities at your feet. I pray that I will seek your righteousness first. Lord, let me be more concerned about building up your kingdom instead of worrying about my faults. Steer my heart away from putting myself down, and allow me to operate from a position of love and care. Lord, let me be as gentle with myself as you are with me. These things I pray in Jesus' name. Amen!

Self-Care

"Self-care and self-love are vital when "adulting", don't neglect taking care of yourself first."

Slow...Down!

Ever feel like you're speeding through life at 80 miles per hour? Well, I have! In the past, I'd become hyper-focused on a certain project and it consumed my life. I suffered headaches that would exert all the motivation out of me. I committed to unrealistic expectations, which often exhausted me. I worked long hours, stopped working out, and barely ate. My productivity caused me to lose sight of the task at hand.

I understand if you're grinding to finish school or pounding the pavement for internships. Every once in awhile, though, take a moment to enjoy the fruits of your labor. Ever sprint a marathon? I don't want to say it's impossible, but it seems pretty far-fetched. The faster you go, the quicker you burn out. This chapter will uncover the power of self-care and self-awareness. I'm slowly working on tending to the needs of Jasmine. I hope this chapter will help you learn to slow down and trust God in your daily grind.

Casper, Wyoming

If you don't slow down, God or your body (sometimes both) will cause you to slow down. This happened to me while driving to Cheyenne, WY, with my little sister. I decided to visit my best friend and book a hair appointment. (If you've ever lived in the Northwest, you know the struggle.) Anyhow, I was driving 80 mph (the speed limit), and my car started to slow down out of nowhere. We went from 80 mph to 0 mph in a matter of seconds. Scary.

We pulled over to the side of the road, thankfully without an accident (Praise Jesus!), and started praying. After troubleshooting and more prayer, we were able to drive 40 mph to the nearest gas station, and then we were well on our way...or so we thought. Twenty miles from the gas station, my car did the same thing again. I knew something was wrong. A tow truck towed my car and we found a safe place to rest.

Slow down and enjoy life!

God wanted me to slow down that day. The whole purpose of the trip was to relax, but I was rushing and not enjoying the quality time with my sister or the beautiful plains of Wyoming. How good is our God? Even in the middle of a not-so-fun situation, He shows us the beauty and the lesson we need at that exact moment!

Years later, my sister brought up this story. I am thankful that we can laugh at the situation now. I'm sure she will tell her kids about the time Auntie Jasmine got on her knees to pray on the highway in the middle of Casper, Wyoming. Slow down and enjoy life! My faith in God allowed me to breathe a little easier in this situation. My emergency fund also helped because when I received the bill for the car maintenance, car rental, and an unexpected hotel stay, I had no idea how I would pay it all. It was faith and previous financial preparation.

Finding Faith

This section may not be for you, but it must be included. I'm not going to preach to you and say I attended church every Sunday while in college because I'd be lying. (Bedside Baptist, anyone? Can I get an Amen?) I am thankful for the messages I did receive while in college. However, I didn't follow Jesus until after graduation. I didn't realize who my maker was and how he had blessed me so richly throughout my lifetime.

I know the struggle of not having enough money for rent and food. At times, I slept on friends' couches because it was a choice between the couch or living in my car. It was not an enjoyable experience, but it made me the person I am today. I was broke, and my selfless friend purchased my textbooks for me because I was in danger of failing a class. I was the girl who couldn't afford textbooks during her junior year of college. Now I'm a 29-year-old, a faithful monthly tither, a two-time homeowner, and an avid investor with no student loan debt. Faith is a beautiful thing. Whatever situation you're going through, that situation will pass. I cannot predict when or how, but I believe that God has a way. Stay humble, trust the process, and keep pushing toward your goals.

I pray every morning, every evening, and throughout the day. I talk to God about what is going on. Usually, after a vent session, I feel better about the situation. I have a devotional on my nightstand and at my work desk. I also go to sleep when I am overwhelmed.

I recognize that I cannot do this life by myself. God has given me everything I need and has never failed me. I am trusting in his wisdom to provide in every area of my life. Is it easy? No. But I know with constant prayer and supplication, my faith will grow stronger in him.

Peace

Self-care and self-love are vital when "adulting," so don't neglect taking care of yourself first. If you're starting your college search, the first semester at school, or your first job, don't forget about your peace. Take time for yourself. Know that the work will always be there, so don't stress too much. Commit to being the best version of yourself daily. Navigate through the adversity, and pick up the pieces when things fall. Create boundaries for work, school, family, relationships, and friends.

Boundaries are a great thing! It establishes who I am to others and reassures me of my peace. I used to think that I was causing issues with boundaries until I started losing my peace. Now I communicate my likes and dislikes to people, and I pray they respect my concerns. If they don't, I kindly remind them of my boundaries. If they still don't comply, I pray for discernment and recognize I may need to move on without them. Why? Because they didn't respect my boundaries, which means they ultimately don't respect me. I try to reciprocate this behavior with my friends, family, co-workers, and church mates. I'm not perfect, but I think it's necessary when adulting.

Drawing the Line

These boundaries can be implemented through methods of organization and time management. While I was in college, my daily planner managed my schedule. I scheduled everything from appointments and homework to eating, grocery shopping, and parties. You name it, and it was in my planner. This is how I managed my life in college and even now as a young professional.

I scheduled time for yoga, walking, or some form of exercise. Imagine being a freshman on a Division 1 track team, an ROTC cadet, and taking 16 credit hours. Holy cow! When did I have time to sleep? Staying on track with a planner allowed me to stay focused on my goals (graduating and commissioning). It also created boundaries so I didn't overbook my time.

Currently, my Fridays are my maintenance days. I check my mail, grocery shop, have a hair appointment, get a pedicure, and relax and enjoy a movie. Wednesday nights are Bible study days, and Sunday mornings are reserved for church. These days are non-negotiable. Of course, life happens when I can't attend either, but these days are programmed and occur like clockwork. They are needed for my spiritual and mental health. I need these days to maintain the vision God has for me. I schedule around these days to prevent any conflict.

"I sit on my floor daily and introspect. I analyze the day and ponder about what I could have improved upon. (This takes about 30 minutes—no more than that though.) I also work out at least four times a week. I attempt to go to bed by 9 p.m. every evening. Every month, I treat myself to a massage and a pedicure. These are habits that have improved my life. I'm not sure how you de-stress, but it's important to take care of yourself! Through my faith, I regained peace that only comes from above. I also found ways to maintain my peace, which resulted in weekly routines of exercising, going to bed early, and monthly pampering sessions."

Vision Boards

Habakkuk 2:2 ""And the Lord answered me and said, 'Write the vision, and engrave it so plainly upon tablets that everyone who passes may read it easily and quickly as he hastens by.'"

I love that God calls us to action. He gives us the vision, but it's our responsibility to write it down and make it plain. Have you ever made a vision board?

Vision boards are tangible pictures that represent the goals you desire to accomplish. Once completed, the board hangs in a visible part of your home or workspace (similar to your financial goals mentioned in chapter 2). This board is a constant reminder of the goals you're working towards.

While in college, my vision board displayed me becoming a fully commissioned officer with the rank of Second Lieutenant, a graduation cap, money, healthy foods, and a picture of a church. These visuals represented my career goals, upcoming graduation, a growing savings account, healthy living, and my desire to strengthen my faith in the Lord. Guess what? I accomplished all of my goals that year. I became a Second Lieutenant, saved over $12,000, ate relatively healthy, and attended church and Bible study regularly.

I encourage you to do this activity with a group of friends or family members. When you write goals down, you gain power through writing. Written goals usually become accomplished goals. The more you speak about your goals, the more people can hold you accountable. But don't run and tell everyone. I'm going to make some suggestions about whom to tell in the next chapter.

Two years ago, six of my closest friends decided to create a goal challenge. We pledged $40 a person to whoever accomplished the most goals. Throughout the year, we updated each other about our goals and progress. This year was even better. We created 10 realistic and measurable goals and are using the $40 pledges to create a scholarship for one woman of color achieving her goals. Our simple goal challenge transformed from helping ourselves and keeping each other accountable into helping someone in our community.

With Vision Comes an Audience

Whenever a new movie or TV show debuts, critics judge the movie or show's elements. They judge the storyline, the acting, the concept, etc. These judgments produce reviews that promote a favorable or unfavorable rating. These critics create a response that influences the world. Their critique can make or break a film. Your vision will solicit an audience, whether you like it or not.

Ever heard of the story of Joseph and his multicolored coat? God gave him a vision of becoming a great leader. Joseph excited about his vision shared it with his jealous brothers. They tried to destroy his vision, however, it worked out for Joseph's good. (**See Genesis**

50:20.) His vision attracted an audience because he was excited about the vision God gave him.

Like Joseph's brothers, some people don't want to hear about your vision. Your vision may intimidate them, so they try to do everything in their power to deter you from this vision. We'll talk about those kinds of people in a later chapter. But for now, be uncomfortable with your vision, and know that people are watching—and that's okay. Let them watch. Greatness is forming! An audience enables both constructive and destructive criticism. One group builds you up, and the other group tears you down.

Feedback is imperative to our overall progress and growth. I recommend self-assessing quarterly. Ask yourself, "Am I where I wanted to be three months ago? Have I created any habits I do not like? Have I committed myself to the goals on my vision board? Will I be where I want to be in the next two years? Five years? Ten years?" Self-assessing your progress will serve as a reminder to keep progressing toward your goals. I love my friends because they are great judges of character but also the goal police. They remind me of a goal I mentioned months ago that I haven't attempted. I enjoy the accountability, even when I don't want to hear it.

The Bridge of No Return

Do you have close friends from elementary or high school? If so, I applaud you. I keep in touch with two people from high school. Yes, only two. Why only two? Because of me! When I was growing up, I had an attitude problem and entitlement issues. I felt like the world owed me something. Because of this attitude, I lost valuable people in my life. After high school, I learned the value of others. We're not going to like everyone we meet, and not everyone is going to like us.

If all the people in the world had similar traits, the world would be a boring place. God created humans in his image. Therefore, your "enemy" was created with God's characteristics, just like you.

Burning Bridges

I advise against burning bridges. Burning bridges will cause more harm than good. We need one another. We can't make it through this world alone. I wish I had known this truth in high school and college; I would have done things differently. I learned from my mistakes, and I encourage you not to make these same mistakes. The bridges formed in high school, college, and on the job can create opportunities and expand your network and net worth like never before. Holding grudges or having enemies is not worth the sorrow or distress. Be mindful of your present and future. You never know who you will need, who will need you, or when you might need each other.

Unrealistic Expectations

As humans, we set expectations for our families, friends, significant others, co-workers, and classmates. When those individuals don't meet our expectations, we sometimes react as if it's the end of the world. (I'm guilty of it.) We are all created differently and should accept each other's differences.

Here's how I set people up for failure with my unrealistic expectations: I direct a scenario and watch it play out in my head. I cast the characters, rewrite the plot, and develop the storyline without input from others. As the scene plays out, unscripted, I am disappointed with the outcome. The problem is unrealistic expectations. Things happen and people won't react or operate in the manner you desire them to. When we want things to pan out a certain way, we are trying to control the narrative and manipulate the person. Control is not love! Control is selfish and inconsiderate of the other person's emotions, thoughts, and personality.

> *"Control is not love! Control is selfish and inconsiderate of the other person's emotions."*

Break Up to Make Up

My high school best friend and I didn't speak to each other for four years after college. After the hiatus, we slowly began communicating, and she and her future husband celebrated an important milestone in my life. I wasn't expecting her to attend, let alone bring me a gift. A few months later, she asked me to be her bridesmaid. I was shocked. I cried because I didn't think I would be invited to the wedding, let alone be a bridesmaid. You never know what God has in store. If the season is over, let it go peacefully, and maybe just maybe, if it's God's will, the person will return when you least expect it.

Breakups suck! I have had my share of breakups, and if you're twenty-something, you probably have too. I've had breakups with friends and boyfriends, and I hate it. I take the majority of the blame because I know I am a challenging person. I have high standards, love hard, am super loyal, and have had issues with control and feedback.

I have had four major breakups (only one was with someone I was romantically involved with) in my life that all resulted in growth. This is a tough reality, yet even in its chaos, it's still beautiful because growth occurred.

> If you're not impacting the positive growth of an individual and vice versa, I think it's best for both parties to move on." Proverbs 27:17 "As iron sharpens iron; so, a man sharpens another."

> In this scripture, it shows the results of effectiveness. Notice it reads, "A man sharpens another." This implies that both are sharpening or have the means to sharpen one another.

Moving on is a part of life. Look at our Savior. He had to move on and sacrifice His life on the cross to save us and allow us to share the gospel. There are times when letting go is healthy for both involved parties. It's heartbreaking and scary, but it's necessary. The world can be a tough place, but it can also be fun. I've made peace with the heartbreaks, and I'm still here to share the story (at least my side).

I encourage you if you've never lived away from home, venture out! There's a whole world out there for you to explore. Make friends, date (if you're into that), make as many mistakes as you can, and learn from it all. The world is at your fingertips. Leave the nest, and start making decisions that will impact your present and your future. It's terrifying at first, but with the power of Christ, a strong support network, and a will to do more than what you think you are capable of, you can do anything! Christ is with you every step of the way.

P.S. Don't Let Their Problems Become Yours

If your friend confides in you, ask them to pray. If they're unwilling, go to God (by yourself), and release their issues. Ask God to send the right person into their lives to minister to them. If it's a tough issue and they're still lost, ask your friend to fast so you can both seek God together.

Life is hard and complicated. There is no sense in taking on more problems that don't concern you. I'm not saying you should be less of a friend; I'm saying I've been through plenty of situations that have cost me health issues, friendships, work relationships, and money because I let other people's problems become my problems. You don't have to be the solution when God is the answer. I have no idea what his plan is, but I do know what his Word says and what he has promised. Remember, you can bring a person to church, but it's up to them to receive Christ as their Lord and Savior. **(See 1 Thess. 4:10-12.)**

I Love Me Some Me!

Do you love you? Are you your biggest hype man? I now accept how silly and reserved I can be. Sometimes I can be messy, and other times I am an organized neat freak with a hint of disorganized chaos. It's hard to explain; I'm paranoid when things aren't in their proper place, but I still cause a mess every once and awhile.

"I value the woman God has created and shaped me to be. I now love myself unconditionally."

Overall, I value the woman God has created and shaped me to be. I love myself unconditionally. I recognize I make mistakes, and prayerfully, I won't make them again. I don't need anyone's approval or chastisement of how they think I should be. The Lord has blessed me with unique dreams and visions, and I wouldn't change those blessings for the world. Start learning to accept yourself unapologetically. People can see when you love yourself. It will exude from your heart, and the light reflected cannot be extinguished.

Being Unapologetically You

Be blessed. Be confident in the person you're becoming. Love yourself, and don't settle for less than God's best. He made promises to you in his Word that he will provide and care for you:

> **You don't need validation from your boss, friends, society, or family. Be comfortable with where you are, wherever God has you.**

> **Isaiah 43:2,4 "When you go through deep waters, I will be with you. When you go through rivers of difficulty, you will not drown…you are precious to me"**

Look in the mirror. I'm serious—look. Say to yourself, 'I am beautiful just the way I am! God created me in his image.' Never stop loving yourself. Period. When you reach the point where you love yourself more than anything, you are comfortable. You don't have to be more or less; you can be you! You can attend a concert by yourself and have the absolute best time. You learn the things you're willing to compromise on and things you won't change. I encourage you today to ask God to show you not only the love he has for you but to show you how you're supposed to love yourself.

Are there areas in my life that need work? Absolutely. Do I think I should be better with my attitude? Yes. (Ughhh, my future daughter will give me a run for my money. I just know it!) I love the woman

I'm becoming and I'm totally fine with the quirks and complexities of my personality. I love Jasmine and I'm learning to do a better job of taking care of me. Every day I learn something new about myself. I know that God is purposefully revealing these details to me. He is the ultimate caregiver and through his instruction and guidance, I can maintain the peace he desires for me. I ray you find peace for yourself, too.

A PRAYER ABOUT SELF-CARE

Heavenly Father, my most precious dove, my protector, and my redeemer, I pray that you would sanctify and bless me. Arm me with the knowledge that I need to survive and prosper. Let nothing separate me from you, O God! I pray for peace over the circle that surrounds me. I pray for supportive and encouraging friends who will push me to new heights. Lord, surround me with your love, and raise me up to be a soldier of the truth. Let me learn to properly care for myself so that I may share that same care, if not more, to others. Lord, I pray the blood of Jesus over me and your saints! Bless us forever. In Jesus' Name, Amen.

Dreamers, Dream Catchers & Dream Killers

> *"As dreamers, we must remember that God hears our dreams and will give us the desires of our hearts, according to His will."*

YOUR DREAMS SHOULD SCARE you, but if they don't, that's okay too. It's important to dream, but it's more important to take action. So many creative and talented people miss out on their dreams. Why? Because they were too scared to do it, or they let the words of others quiet their dreams. In this chapter, we'll discuss dreamers, dream catchers, and dream killers. Everyone needs to dream and make their dreams a reality. After all, that is the purpose of a dream (in my opinion).

Dreamers

Dreamers are individuals who can be characterized as ambitious, creative, and hardworking. If an idea pops into their head, they will figure out a way to accomplish it. They love their dreams and will do anything to reach them. This may be you. *Congrats!* If this isn't you, ask yourself, "Why am I not dreaming?" Have you stalled on a vision that God has placed in your heart? Run toward those moments where you felt inspired and challenged. In that space, you will find your dream.

While growing up, I knew someday I'd be someone of importance. I prepared my speech for the Academy Awards and could engage in a monologue from one of my favorite plays. It was a dream I chased for years. I aspired to be an actress in high school. The expression that stemmed from "Tall" aided my journey to acting. Instead of pursuing acting, I took a chance and decided to play volleyball throughout high school. Unfortunately, I didn't play in college, but the discipline I learned in volleyball proved beneficial for my life. Life isn't perfect and sometimes your plans will shift. However, failing plans could result in a beautiful future. I didn't become a successful Hollywood actress (yet), but I explored other opportunities in my life. I went to school for film, worked in the entertainment industry, then realized that I desired to establish other goals. At the time, I thought importance meant having a star on Hollywood Blvd. While this is an amazing accomplishment for a selective bunch, it wasn't the only way to achieve a level of importance. I now work as a financial officer, execute multi-million dollar budgets, and have traveled to the Middle East and Asia to serve my country. Serving is important to me and that's what counts.

Sometimes dreamers will chase a dream without remembering to shift. Imagine having dreams of becoming a veterinarian but you don't like dogs or cats and you fall asleep during standardized tests. Maybe you might be chasing after the wrong vision of the dream. It could be that the dream is to help animals in a different capacity.

It's okay to tweak your vision. This is perfectly normal. Not everything will go according to plan. Through careful analysis, I'd recommend recognizing your shortfalls and altering your plans to produce results. God knows the plans He has for us. Even if we're unsure, God makes it clear that He will give us a future and a hope. **(See Jer. 29:11.)**

My mission in life is to serve God, advance the kingdom, and become a loving, caring, and compassionate woman. **How do I plan to obtain this?** By working hard at my job, building the kingdom of God, daily displaying Jesus, and becoming the best woman I can be in this moment. In everything, I want to glorify Him. I wrote this vision down as a reminder for when I get distracted or distracted to keep pressing toward the vision.

I have a passion for education. I don't always focus when I need to, but I love learning. I aspire to expand my mind and gain knowledge daily. That's how I knew college was for me. I didn't know where I wanted to attend, but I knew that obtaining an education was part of the plan. I didn't start researching colleges until my sophomore year of high school, and even then, I didn't apply until senior year. I was nervous about rejection, leaving home, and trying something new. What if I fail? The best part of a dream is that it's something you've never done before and now you have the opportunity to make it come true. Failing is part of the process toward success.

When I applied to colleges, I ensured my transcripts were mailed on time, diversified my extra-curricular activities, and perfected my personal statements. I didn't want anything to get in the way of attending college. I encountered stumbling blocks along the way, but I went to college and finished early. Keep chasing the dream, and don't let anything get in your way!

Dream Catchers

"I've learned that people will forget what you said, people will forget what you did, but people will never forget how you made them feel." - Maya Angelou

Dream catchers are individuals who listen to dreamers and cultivate these dreams. They receive dreams and equip the dreamer with the tools required to build upon their dreams. This support can range from mental to spiritual, financial, and/or personal assistance. Dream catchers can be mentors, teachers, parents, or even strangers.

Have you ever seen a dream catcher? It was originally made by North American Indians that essentially catches good dreams. You hang them over your bed, and while you're sleeping, the catcher is supposed to catch dreams. The dreams are to remain in the catcher until they are made true. Your dream catcher can be anyone; they can be key individuals or random strangers in your life that motivate you to chase your dreams.

Catching Sweet Dreams

Last year, I booked a sugaring appointment. Sugaring is a form of hair removal that offers a more natural and less painful hair removal process.

I walked into Green City Studios in Philadelphia, PA, and met my sugarista, Ashley. She was so warm and welcoming. As she ventured to my most delicate places for sugaring (too much information, I know), she opened up about her story. She mentioned how she worked in corporate America after college. She left her 9–5 to start Green City Studios. I was amazed at her ability, poise, transparency, and gracefulness. She was so excited about my journey. Ashley encouraged me to finish this book and mentioned how our stories were similar. She is a great example of a dream catcher. Her words became a catalyst to press on with my entrepreneurial ventures. Thank you, Ashley!

Dream catchers recognize the importance of cultivating a dream and will encourage others to push toward their dreams. You should have a few dream catchers in your circle that believe in you and will cultivate your dreams.

> *"The fulfillment of dreams requires ambition, patience,*
> *a strong support system, resources, and faith."*

My baby sister loves cooking food. She will do anything to get her hands on the next recipe. She is 16 years old, and I think she believes her age will pause her goals and aspirations. When she was 10, I gifted her with a celebrity chef cooking event. She went to a five-star kitchen and learned how to prepare a three-course meal. Years later, she cooks and bakes better than some of the chefs on cooking shows. (I am biased, of course, but she's really good.) She even started her own baking business. In a way, I think I maybe her dream catcher. She's an artist, a baker, a chef, a dog lover, and an athlete. I encourage her to use her talents as much as possible. I believe in her; she is so gifted. I push her to be the best version of herself every day.

It's not about size, age, education, or socioeconomic status. Dreams don't discriminate. The fulfillment of dreams requires ambition, patience, a strong support system, resources, and faith. A dream catcher exposes the dreamer to their talents. Keep your dream catchers close and your dream killers far away.

Dream Killers

Dream killers do exist, so be on guard. These individuals are doubters or naysayers or don't say anything at all. What do I mean? Let's say you have a great idea or dream. The person you share it with says, "Okay." You are excited and expect this person to embrace your excitement. Instead, they remain silent. They never mention the dream unless you bring it up. They don't follow up on the progress of your dream either. Truthfully, reader, I'd caution surrounding yourself with anyone who doesn't cultivate your dreams and visions. If they're not celebrating you or pushing you forward, why are you allowing them to dim your light?

My dreams are often unexplainable, far-fetched, and a bit odd. That's the great thing about believing in God because he does the impossible. He birthed Jesus through a virgin, enabled a donkey to talk, made barren women pregnant, and raised a dead man. There's nothing too big for him. I've learned not everyone has an active imagination as I do. But that's okay. I tell people, "Well, this is how God created me, and I believe him for this." Those who may oppose your dream could attack the vision God has placed on your heart.

These dream killers might not want to intentionally hurt you, but their words and actions can be cancerous. They will doubt you and say things like "This is in your best interest. You probably shouldn't do that. I have never seen anyone accomplish it." Stay true to yourself and your dream. Be firm in your goals and conviction, and remember who always provides.

I find it interesting when individuals tell me I can't do something or suggest to me that my goals are "too big." How can anyone see a dream that they did not conceive? If God gave me the vision, why hinder that vision? I don't want to mislead you. There are vector checks that people should provide. If you're about to jump off a cliff, please seek godly counsel. There will always be someone telling you that you can't do anything. I say, "Go for it!" (as long as it is safe, legal, and makes you happy). If you fail, at least you tried. If you need to alter your dream, go back to the drawing board, learn from your mistakes, and try, try again.

A few years ago, I had the opportunity to invest in real estate. Before making the decision, I prayed, solicited financial advisors, and shared my dream with a few friends and a few strangers. It was a risky decision, but I figured I had no immediate responsibilities or debt except my rental property mortgage. A trusted confidant informed me that my decision was a poor choice and tried to talk me out of it. I was concerned and prayed about it even more. I started doubting myself. Want to know the crazy part? The individual never invested in anything comparable.

I encourage you to listen to people who don't agree with you. Why? Because they offer differing opinions. Sometimes hearing the truth from an outsider may be what you need to hear, even if it goes against what you believe (in reason). Understand that your family and friends will not always agree with you, but they should support you. Discern the conversation. Ask Is this beneficial or is the other person lacking knowledge and therefore attempting to disrupt my dreams? Be bold and own it. Ultimately, you have to live with the decision.

I always wanted to purchase real estate. In college, I didn't have the resources or the knowledge to purchase a home. After I gradua-ted, I saved toward a house. I told a few people about my dreams to buy a home, and I instantly received negative feedback. "Why do you want to live here forever? It's expensive. You're too young.

Renting is so much easier..." and the list goes on. The people who saw my visión supported me and are the same people who continue to support me today.

I thought my dream was dying after I kept hearing the negativity and had zero luck with the home search. I broke down and rented an apartment for a year while I kept saving. My goal was to find a home before my lease ended. I took care of this goal like a baby. My hours after work was dedicated to home-buying. On my way home from work, I stopped by properties and observed the surrounding areas. I also shut my mouth. Initially, when the dream was fresh, I shared it with everyone. I went back to the drawing board, tweaked the goal, and silently made moves.

Don't Settle

The end of September neared, and I still hadn't found a house. (My lease ended in December.) Due to the pressure of not finding a house, I settled and put an offer on a house. Rule #1: Don't settle!

I became extremely anxious. I knew I would be nervous about buying a home, but this was a "not so good nervous." Every time I walked into the house, I couldn't picture myself living there. It required over $20K in repairs, which was something I didn't have at the time. After much prayer, I released it to God. I backed out of the home. The house was dreadful. The beautiful exterior couldn't mask the outdated interior. From a moldy basement to cat urine-infested carpets, I couldn't believe this was the road I was headed down. Any counterfeit will prove itself. You don't have to look hard. The evidence will usually be right in front of your face.

The house needed so much work, and (deep down I knew) I desired a move-in-ready home. After changing realtors and praying,

I continued to hear negativity. I went back to the drawing board and prayed even more. A few days later, I found my home outfitted with hardwood floors, brand new carpet, new paint, an attached garage, a basement, and a fenced-in yard. It possessed EVERYTHING I wanted. The only problem I encountered was that it was $10K over my budget. I started thinking maybe the dream killers were right. Maybe I couldn't afford this house. Maybe I was in over my head.

In times when I feel over my head, I am encouraged because God is an "in over my head" kind of God. He blesses beyond measure when we least expect it. I went to God with my realtor and pastor and we prayed in the home three times. I revamped my budget and I could afford more than my initial budget. I consulted financial advisors and they recommended I go for it. They told me, "Live in a home that makes you happy and one you can afford too." I did just that! I moved into my home eight days before my lease ended. The dream killers couldn't defeat me this time, and they never will. During this time of worry and confusion, I was reminded of asking and receiving, seeking and finding, knocking and doors opening. **(See Matt. 7:7.)**

As dreamers, we must remember that God knows our dreams and will give us the desires of our hearts, according to his will. Dream killers don't see your vision. They believe that you are not capable of accomplishing what you desire, no matter how good, educated, blessed, or talented you are. Do not let these individuals get the best of you. They are placed in your path to empower you, not to tear you down. If your heart is set on something, go for it. Other's attempts to bring you down should be used as fuel to work harder. Prove not only to them but also to yourself that you can keep pushing toward your goals. The world is yours, so go out there and take it (and of course make it a better place).

A PRAYER FOR DREAMERS

God, you have big plans not only for my future but for your kingdom. I desire more now than I did before. I pray that my dreams will come true in your holy will. I pray that I will be surrounded by other dreamers and catchers. I pray for the dream that I am struggling to uncover. I pray you would wow me like never before. I pray you will start a fire in my heart that will continue to roar. Let my expectations exceed anything I could ever imagine! I pray that I will boldly act on my dreams. With the discernment of the Holy Spirit and through faith, I pray I will press forward in any assignment you bring to me. I pray you will protect my dreams and allow them to come true. Keep them near to me, Lord. In your Son's Name, Amen.

Experience, Trials & Triumph

"There's someone out there who needs to hear and see you. They need your gifts."

INTERNSHIPS ARE A BEST-KEPT secret. High-paying jobs today require a degree and field-related experience. You're probably wondering, how the heck am I supposed to get experience when I am taking 16 credit hours a semester?

I've thought about interning even now, while I am employed full-time. Why? Because internships keep you fresh. You can make mistakes without fear of losing a paycheck. You can learn from other people in your industry of interest. Internships also tell you a lot about yourself and your work ethic.

Throughout college, I interned at five different organizations. Some were non-profits; others were for-profit. Two were paid, three were unpaid. The life lessons learned couldn't be taught in the classroom. For example, I learned the more I became interested in the task at hand, the better the result. I couldn't just sit behind a computer screen for hours; if I did, I needed to be on some type of social media site. That's why I became a social media coordinator for two of my internships. I got paid to create content and launch social media accounts. My first internship required operating on social media platforms and preparing public relations packages. I loved these internships because they challenged me and allowed me to have fun.

Working for Free

I worked in the entertainment and performing arts industry and found little to no paid internships. Many companies that I came across wanted to hire new talent and train them but didn't have a budget for hired help. The compensation is the experience gained on the job, a potential credit, or more contacts in the industry. Don't shy away from unpaid internships. They may work in your favor.

Don't get me wrong, receiving minimal compensation for the number of hours and effort worked, especially when working in Manhattan, was challenging. However, I wouldn't have changed it for the world. Some days, I had to dig deep to find the strength and courage to enter the company. Funny enough, I have to find the same strength and courage to go to work now. See how previous experience helps? The unpaid experience molded my work ethic to succeed in my current career. If I can get up to go to work for free, I can certainly wake up refreshed and ready for my six-figure salary.

Yes, it stinks not getting paid, especially when your friends are working summer jobs. But at this moment, look past the money and think of the experience you will gain while at this temporary position. Yes, I say a moment because it's just a moment. You will create many more moments in the future. I have memories of rooftop parties in NYC, getting lost in Philadelphia, filming a celebrity-filled jam session in Durham, and meeting globally known dance choreographers, just to name a few. I have made friends and mentors whom I contact regularly. Make it fun, make it count, and make it last.

My lack of qualifications encouraged me to fight for the experience. Never count yourself out! I wouldn't have attained the level of success I have today if I did. I am not saying apply to every internship or job on the planet, but let others to unlock the potential in you that you might not see. I fight for experience and I fight to get in the door. Too often we doubt ourselves and our abilities. We must remember that we are God's children and that He makes no mistakes. We are the ultimate Creator's creation. Therefore, we must believe that God, through his strength, will be with us every step of the way.

I found my first internship on social media using #internshipnyc and found a communications internship for a non-profit company in NYC. I sent my resume and cover letter immediately. The next day, I received a call requesting a phone interview. After the interview, the owner hired me and my first day would be in the following weeks.

Nineteen-year-old me was headed to the Big Apple for my first internship. The experiences from that first internship led to an abundance of opportunities and growth. I was living in one of the best cities in the world and befriended some cool females—one of whom will share her story with you in the epilogue.

The production manager at the non-profit company and hired me as her social media manager the following summer. My unpaid internship turned into being a social media manager to the 2011 Ladies of Hip-Hop Festival program coordinator. Here I was, 20 years old, managing a $5,000 crowdfunding campaign and working with top choreographers from around the world. It also landed me a mentor for life, Michele Byrd-McPhee, owner of Ladies of Hip-Hop Festival.

My first internship pushed me to broaden my skills in public relations—an area of communications that didn't interest me. I edited and distributed press releases, assisted with event planning, created contact lists, and more. I had very little experience, but it allowed me to explore areas outside of my comfort zone. This experience set me up for later internships that landed me projects in my current position and throughout the community.

> *"We must remember that we are God's children and He made no mistakes."*

Now, I am very meticulous and believe that a product reveals a thousand words. The more time you invest in the neatness of the product, the more people will invest in it as well.

Money Flow

I had goals of saving money as I prepared for my final semester. I knew I had to secure a paid internship. After applying to 35 internships and receiving negative responses, I finally received an interview with the former chief of staff at a large international airport. Because of the number of internships I had applied to, I forgot what the job description entailed. (They removed the job description from their website before I had a chance to review it.) However, this was my only phone call for the summer. I printed off my resume and headed for the interview a week later.

The chief of staff met me at the company's lobby. We shared pleasantries, and she opened the conversation with "Why do you think you're qualified for this position?" Oh, geez, the one question I didn't have prepared. I took a deep breath and told her, "I am versed in marketing, film, leadership, social media, digital media, and public relations. I have a diverse background and am ready and willing to learn the skills necessary for the position. I hope that by the end of the summer, I will have exceeded your expectations and will walk away with a job."

I was hired on the spot. She was so impressed with my resume, my experience, and my former positions that she created a job just for me. I became her executive assistant. At the age of 20, I worked with the number two senior-ranking officers at a major international airport. Although I felt under-qualified, God strategically designed the position for me.

I was assigned to the airport's strategic business plan team, social media team, and disaster relief program. This is my testimony to you that dreams can come true. We created press releases, launched social media platforms, and reached a global audience. I incorporated the skills and experiences learned from my first internship to grow and develop the strategy within this new position.

With the help of engineers, lawyers, analysts, and experts, I formulated a natural disaster plan for the airport that is currently implemented today. At the time, I had no idea what I was doing, but my leadership trusted me with figuring it out. I entered rooms I had no business in. It was uncomfortable being surrounded by subject matter experts, but I needed them and they needed me. This internship developed my determination and work ethic.

Getting Paid

I've had two paid internships and one derived from an unpaid internship. I remember putting in long hours and sleepless nights for both unpaid and paid internships. Why? Because my name was attached to them.

I did my best every day because of three things:

1. a potential job offer,
2. a reliable referral,
3. excellence, which is required for success.

Paid internships meant I was a part of the team because I was on the payroll. Every two weeks a check was deposited into my account. Fulfillment of payment came with responsibilities. Being on the payroll required discipline and effort. The company expected its employees to adhere to their policies and, most importantly, the job description. My paycheck was an agreement that I would deliver on-time results. Remember, you're a representation of the organization, so your actions and work reflect on the company.

Both unpaid and paid internships were valuable as I learned from my supervisors and co-workers. I am grateful for all the experience I obtained, and the paid internships allowed me to save and prepare for life after graduation.

Both types of internships are great resume builders. You can gain a wealth of experience and networking opportunities from any internship. If you're making minimum wage, remember, this internship isn't forever. I survived to live in NYC with a $200 MetroCard and a $300 monthly stipend. Learn as much as you can, maximize your resources, and live a little. You will survive. These unique opportunities will shape and craft your purpose.

Beyond internships

Volunteering allows you to sharpen other skills, such as followership, teaching, organization, and project management and allows you to give back to your community. Whether you're in college or not, I recommend volunteering in areas unrelated to your interests. I encourage you to give outside of your normal circle to touch other's lives and for your life to be touched in the process.

During my freshman year, I tutored third and fourth graders. I never tutored young people before, but I learned so much from them. They were eager to learn and always wanted to have fun.

My mentee, Avery[3], motivated to impact more youth. Avery's home wasn't the most supportive and through our tutoring sessions, we learned from one another. I was sensitive to her home life and knew our time together was a moment of peace for her. (I think this is where I started liking kids.) My heart broke for her and the many children who didn't receive the love and care they deserve at home. Avery and I formed a bond that was vital for her growth and mine. I considered her to be like my little sister and a blessing to me.

The same year, I helped register voters in my first voter-eligible presidential election. It was 2008. I immersed myself in everything politics, from campaigning to market strategy to polling stations. I believed then and now that our right to vote is powerful. We have an opportunity to reach the world. Throughout my local college area, I spoke to strangers thirty to forty years older than I was about

---

3   Some names and identifying details have been changed to protect the privacy of individuals.

the importance of voting. Some had never voted before and decided to register. They said if I was bold enough to walk the streets and encourage voters, the least they could do was vote. Talk about encouraging! I was 18 and impacting change in our country. I was empowered, excited, and passionate to share the message.

How can you change the world right now? Imagine yourself making an impact right now, whether you're 16, 18, or 27. If you did it now, what would the world be like when you're 50? Right now, an organization is looking for a person like you. I encourage you to try something new, to stretch past the familiar and give back. There's someone out there who needs to hear and see you. They need your gifts.

Experience is found everywhere. Opportunities are presented in internships, odd jobs, and volunteer positions. Maybe it's working in your aunt's hair salon on Saturday mornings or planting a community garden or adopting a highway to clean. Seek opportunities and don't be surprised when an opportunity comes knocking on your door.

Application:

- Don't take yourself too seriously. New experiences sharpen your skill set.
- We all learn from making mistakes.
- Build your network, especially from those working alongside you.
- Record your accomplishments. Any projects or work experience will help build your resume.
- Get out of your comfort zone.
- Try something new and do your best.
- Don't like it? Finish what you started and move on.

A PRAYER ABOUT EXPERIENCE

Dear God,

I thank you for being God over my life, over my heart and over my path. You have given me a path to go and Lord I thank you for the challenge. As I walk this path, Lord, let me be obedient to your will God. Lord, even if it doesn't look like how I envisioned it or if it's not exactly where I desire to be, I pray that I will use this experience to the fullest. I pray I will be content in this season. I pray that I will not be bitter or complain, but recognize that you are in every season of my life. Thank you for this opportunity. In Jesus Name, Amen.

The D-Word

I DESIRE TO BE A wife and mother one day, and I do believe the Lord will bless those desires. Dating has shaped my life for the better and, at times, for the worse. I wish I had a magic formula for you to have a great dating life, but I don't. I am no expert, but I believe in love. I've learned how to treat others by loving God and loving myself and my neighbor. Guess what? Love hurts at times. But it's beautiful, it's breathtaking, and it's required. This chapter will discuss my insecurities and failures within the lane of dating. I'm not perfect, and my exes aren't either, but I hope this gives you some insight into the d-word, especially if you're a Christian.

I used to be head over heels about any attractive man—bonus points if he was saved. I recognize now that not every attractive, Christian man is meant to be my husband. I'm sure you're laughing at me, but you've probably done it too. I was so quick to want to run down the altar after "hello." I consumed myself with him and never made room for God. Now I know better, so I do better. Am I married? No. Am I dating? No. Am I content? Yes.

Why is this relevant? My friends and I have experienced heartbreak after heartbreak, and I am sure you have too. It's not fun. As you enter into this new season of college or the professional world, I challenge you to find yourself. God calls individuals first. Our relationship with Him should always begin with and sustain a one-on-one interaction. If you're in a healthy, mutually beneficial, growth-building relationship, then, by all means, continue. If you're single, understand that people enter your life for a season to grow, to sow, to plant, or to water.

Have you read Songs of Solomon? Many examples of love are found in the Bible. God exemplifies this model through the sending of his Son, Jesus Christ. We may not be gleaning the fields like Ruth, but there are plenty of examples within the Bible that can be applied to our own lives.

In Songs of Solomon, the author eloquently pens a beautiful narrative to his bride. The main character is clear that he is awakening love because they desire it. The man is wooing his bride. He pursues her, she recognizes, acknowledges and affirms his pursuit. That's the love I desire[4].

Standard Living

I know God will give me peace about whomever he sends. I don't have to settle for anything less than his best and, honestly, anyone who doesn't cultivate, cover, or nurture my anointing. Okay, maybe it isn't a waste of time, because we are all called to be a light to this dying world. But I have put so much time, effort, and energy into some people when a romantic relationship should have never even been on the table. Save yourself the heartache, and seek God first in all things! He will give you the peace and love that you need that no one else can give! Friend, I encourage you to communicate your

---

4   If you're single or even dating, I recommend reading Mingling of Souls by Matt Chandler. This book cracks the mystery of Songs of Solomon, dating, sex, and marriage.

needs and expectations. Make efforts to maintain or release people depending on the discernment of the Holy Spirit.

Life comes with seasons, just like nature. Ecclesiastes 3:1 "There's a time for everything under the sun and heavens." There are certain people, habits, and circumstances that are meant to sustain every season of your life.

Intentional Living

Imagine your life right now. Imagine you have bills to pay, but you're unintentional about finding work. The results may be an eviction, collections, or unnecessary financial stress. That's what it looks like when people enter unintentional relationships. Entering into unintentional relationships is dangerous and can lead to heartbreak and devastation. The partners of this exchange unintentionally and inadvertently hurt one another because they lack vision. This lack of vision and communication causes confusion, which is not an attribute of God.

Lately, I've stumbled upon far too many young people who involve themselves with other people. They may be attracted to this person but never leave the friend zone or enter into a relationship. The two remain in this fuzzy area of "I like you, but I don't necessarily want to be exclusive with you." Admittedly, I've found myself in confusing situations loosely resembling a relationship.

You do everything for the person, maybe even date them, but for some reason, you both have decided not to label the relationship. Instead, you both aimlessly wander harboring feelings, becoming close, but never defining the relationship or involving God. It's a basket of confusion, sprinkled with lust and foolishness. How did you even end up there?

A few years ago, I felt the Lord calling me to marriage. I moved across the country for a new job, and at the time, it made sense. I wasn't in a relationship, but I received confirmation after confirmation about my future husband (not anyone specific). I continued to pray about it, and a guy appeared. He was nice, cute, and a Christian (kind of). Unfortunately, God is not the only one who hears our prayers and knows our desires; the enemy knows them as well.

Because of my curiosity, I went against everything I believed in and entertained the idea. I experienced red flag after red flag. First, I told everyone about it. Oops. Talk about embarrassing. But this proved to work in my favor. I received strange looks from my closest girlfriends as I shared the weekly update about this guy. They all gave me the "Are you sure about this?" look. My closest girlfriends husbands were curious about this guy to the point where they even called me. (Seek friends with spouses who care about your wellbeing!) This man did not intentionally pursue me. His actions and behavior were passive, sprinkled with sweet sayings. He didn't want to commit to me. He liked the idea of me and enjoyed my company but did not want anything more, especially not a commitment. This lack of commitment left my heart challenged and confused. I was left heartbroken and feeling unworthy. (These are all lies from the enemy.)

"I enjoyed dating myself and learning
how to talk to God again."

After moving past the shame and guilt, I looked to God for counsel. It took me a long time to seek him. Why? Because the situation created so much confusion, and I began to put my trust in this man instead of God. I remember one night he shared that I was too religious. It hurt. So what did I do? Instead of accommodating Jesus, I accommodated the insecurities of this man and dimmed my light. When I stopped talking about God, I started speaking about things that weren't so godly. How could I, a minister, not talk about King Jesus? How could I shy away from the cross? It's embarrassing, but it's the truth. I did it to make someone feel comfortable, but it ultimately made me uncomfortable. It cuts deep and reveals the ugliness inside a person. I couldn't believe I thought I could share my life with someone who didn't also share my love for Jesus and had no desire to strengthen a relationship with him.

Once I worked up enough courage to return to God and repent, I fasted and prayed and instantly received my answer. Wow, talk about hard-hitting! God does not play with his children. I was losing myself and my faith while in this situation. I was relying on this man more than I was relying on God. After my fast, I discerned the Holy Spirit calling me away from this guy. Thank God, he did. This guy was playing me like a fool. Silly me. I chose to awaken love for a man who didn't desire love from me.

Friends, anytime you put your faith and hope in someone or something, you are bound to be hurt and disappointed. Why? Because we are imperfect humans who make mistakes. We were not created to bear the weight of another. When we place our hope and faith in God, we will not be disappointed. He supplies all of our needs.

It was hard to let go, but it was purposeful. Once I spoke the truth about the situation, I regained my strength and peace. You know it's bad when you're not glorifying God or edifying yourself or the body of Christ. I was so interested in having this man's attention that I didn't realize God's attention was more important. I learned after leaving this situation that any man led by God would lead me back to God, not himself.

I thought because I was being "kept," we were supposed to be together. But this man was going to continue to play with me until he was ready to settle down with someone else. That's the thing; a man after God's own heart will not play with his sister in Christ. He understands who she belongs to and will either step up to the plate or leave her alone. The man or woman has to be connected to the Father to understand their rightful position. This person knows that by letting something go, he or she is making room for God's very best.

In this heartbreak season, I re-learned to love Jasmine again and went back to the Word of God. I looked in the mirror and affirmed I am fearfully and wonderfully made (Psalm 139:14). I enjoyed dating myself and learning how to talk to God again.

Don't get me wrong; I was ashamed. I couldn't believe I allowed myself to disrupt my relationship with God, but God's grace is sufficient. He never held it against me. He accepted me with open arms. He never once judged or criticized me, even though I was judging and criticizing myself. How could I be so naive? So gullible? Won't I know the man from God when I see him? God forgives and loves. He loves us exactly where we are and understands that we fall short over and over again.

How I Think I'll Know

He hasn't given up on us and will continue the work in us. Don't judge. I may be wrong about this, but I think I won't miss the very thing God wants for me. Why?

- I would've prayed on it.
- My spouse will encourage my faith walk.
- My spouse will love me like Christ loved the Church.
- My family and friends will recognize Jesus in my spouse.
- More importantly, I'll recognize Jesus in my spouse.

Confused? If you're currently dating and don't know where it's leading, seek God together, but leave room for God by yourself. I know that's one mistake I wish I could rewrite. Once I hurried into a relationship (without consulting God), I would begin to isolate myself from friends and God and immediately spend all my time with my significant other.

Create a balance between spending time with God, family, friends, hobbies, and your significant other. Don't forget the people who were there before this person, and more importantly, don't forget about God! There's a reason why witnesses are needed even for a courthouse wedding. Chew on that for a second. It's important to spend time with your significant other, but there's a balance.

In the past, I've looked at every guy interested in me and whom I was mutually interested in as a potential future spouse. I had our destination wedding planned before we even finished our first date. By the third date, I knew he was "the one." By month six (if we made it that far), it was over, and I was crushed.

How could my future husband leave me like that? Didn't he know the world I created for us in my head? This man wasn't even ready for a commitment, and I felt like we had endured a mini-divorce. I was devastated. After a tub of ice cream, prayer, and binge-watching A Different World, I moved onto another prospect. I'd go through this same vicious cycle of liking, fantasizing, getting hurt, and moving on.

I often felt like Megan Goode in the Oxygen TV movie, *Love by the 10th Date*. Seriously. Goode's character was a hopeless romantic who loved love. However, she rushed into love and never truly learned how to love herself. Throughout the movie, she recharged her love for herself, and her love began to attract others. Spoiler alert! The movie ends with her truly loving and displaying her best self and getting the guy of her dreams. The final scene displays the words "I am enough" written on her hand fills the television screen. She was enough, and so are you! There's a reason why the second greatest commandment is "to love your neighbor as yourself" (Mark 12:31). We have to love ourselves to love others. That's why I stress in previous chapters to establish boundaries, maintain self-care, and be your biggest fan.

My old ways of dating distorted my view of relationships. How could I be so quick to want to marry a guy I just met? Because he thinks I'm cute and intelligent? What? Of course, I'm beautiful and smart. That's a given, but it's not enough to sustain a relationship or even a friendship.

When I meet a female for the first time, I am reserved. We start our acquaintance by going to lunch. I usually don't spend hours on the phone or text them frequently throughout the day. Every few weeks, we may grab a bite to eat in a public place (usually for lunch). I don't immediately invite her to my place until I'm sure she's not crazy. Why do I take it slow with females but kick it into fourth gear with men? Am I the only one who does this?

I listen closely to her responses, and if I see any red flags. If I notice any, I analyze them or figure out my exit strategy. Finally, when we get close enough, we begin to share our baggage, but we're not 100% open. After a few years/trips later, I love her and consider her to be my sister. She's been with me through thick and thin and loves me. We become comfortable with one another and can discern when something is out of place. We challenge each other, and when we disagree, we try to resolve it with love and grace. We pray with each other when life is overwhelming. We keep each other lifted before God in our war room.

Do you see how that works? I wonder how healthier our romantic relationships would be if we approached them like friendships. I know you're probably thinking, but Jasmine, I'm trying to get married. I get it. I am too. I don't know about you, but I want my future husband to be my friend. So as careful as I am with the selection of my girlfriends, I should be even more careful with my future husband. We should learn to discern the heart of our significant other and pray his heart will be focused on God.

Dating Now

My love life is currently under construction. My standards for men have drastically changed. In college, I desired a man with a significant amount of income, who had earned several degrees, who treated me okay, and, more importantly, was well off. In my younger days, this is the kind of man I desired to marry. Do you notice a trend? I had no standard for love, respect, or a relationship with Jesus. He could be the finest thing since sliced bread, but he could also be verbally abusive or spiritually dead. But he made money and provided for our household, so it's all good, right? *Wrong!* In my younger days, I strung men along and broke their hearts. I am ashamed and I truly am sorry. Why would I treat others like this?

Because I had unresolved hurt living and dwelling in my heart. Ever heard the phrase "Hurt people hurt people"? I swam in hurt.

The hurt from my past relationships permeated my spirit, resulting in growing pains and a lack of self-esteem. I didn't know what love was, but anger and I were acquainted, and sadness was a sometimes friend. Expressing love was and still is challenging for me.

In my current relationship with God, I believe he truly loves me. He reveals the junk in my heart. He challenges me to grow and develop into a better woman. Even when I make a mistake, he loves me just the same. I never have to prove my worth to him, because he calls me (and us) worthy (Luke 12: 6–7). That's the kind of relationship I desire with a man. Someone who is forgiving every single day. Someone who loves me beyond the things I can give him. Someone willing to die to his flesh daily and submit to the will of the Lord and me.

Forgiveness

I can't even remember the last time I had a real date. (It's been years!) I know you're probably wondering, How the heck do you plan on a man finding you? I trust God. Don't get me wrong. I don't believe I should stay at my house, waiting for Mr. Right to come knocking on my door. (But anything is possible with God, right?) I do enjoy hanging out. I attend movies, concerts, restaurants, and events, usually by myself. I believe amid my serving and exploring, I will meet a nice (and attractive) man after God's own heart. In the meantime, I can't put life on hold. I did that before, and it's not fun at all.

Living Your Best Life Now

A couple of years ago, I paused in life. I was miserable. I stayed home every weekend, because:

1. I didn't have anyone to hang out with, and
2. I felt like the popular places were not holy enough for me to attend.

Talk about self-righteous! I was so bored and felt my personality slipping from me because I put myself in a box. Friend, if you want to go out, then go out (be safe, of course). Don't trap yourself in a thought process that because you're saved, you can only attend certain events or sit at home. If you're the one that solely attends Christian events, please don't take offense at what I'm about to write. We must enable the lost to develop a relationship with the Father. Those lost souls normally aren't attending your weekly Bible study or local small group.

I love events not centered around the church because it usually stretches me outside of my comfort zone. It allows me to share the love of Jesus with someone who probably doesn't know him. I imagine my marriage ministry will be ministering to the world through our love, marriage, and gifts. Why not get a head start?

1 Cor 7:32 "The unmarried man is anxious about the things of the Lord, how to please the Lord"

Therefore, while we are single, our focus should be pleasing God.

We please God through our actions, love, faith, and works. I know you see everyone around you getting married, birthing babies, buying homes, and traveling the world. I see it too. I'm in Jamaica writing this chapter, and it's beautiful and hopeful to witness couples who are in love. I thank God and pray my marriage is as encouraging and inviting as the marriages of the couples I meet.

The more I read the Bible and cultivate my relationship with God, the more equipped I am to deal with others. God willing, I will marry a man who loves me as Christ loves the Church. I believe my future husband is getting on his knees (right now) praying with and for me, fasting for our family, and preparing to lead our household. I know he has flaws and issues. He is not perfect, and I pray I'm okay with his imperfections and he's okay with mine. Whoever he is, I cannot wait to meet him! I want to share our love with our kids and the world. As I long for love, I remember that forgiveness is love. The Father forgave my sins and yours. Why? Because he loved us first.

PRAYER FOR DATING

Dear God, I pray I will believe and cherish the love you have for me. I pray I will cultivate this love by maintaining a relationship with you. I pray that when I am ready, I will awaken the desire of love boldly. I pray that when I give love to a significant other, co-workers, friends, or family members, that person will receive my love. I pray, Lord, that if they don't receive my love, I will continue to love them anyway. I pray my ministry will revive dead relationships and bring more people to Christ. I pray that you will bond an equal yoke to me at the right time. I pray that once we are yoked, our fruit will nourish the world. I thank you, Lord, in advance for your blessings! In Jesus' Name, Amen.

Being Proud of the New Me

GOD, OF COURSE, DECIDED that view needed a change—an unexpected change. Seven years ago, this chapter would have been nonexistent. The younger me was as free as a bird. That free bird chose to move seven hours away from home to start a new life in North Carolina. That me rarely went home on holidays; I usually rushed off to Europe and mission trips during school breaks. That me barely went home at all. I hated going back home because of the bridges I had burned and my not-so-fond memories of Delaware. When I left at 18, I chose to see the world and keep Delaware in my rearview mirror.

God, of course, decided that view needed a change—an unexpected change. As much I never wanted to set foot in Delaware again (only to visit family), God created a position for me back home at the place where my parents met over 30 years ago. God is so funny. My time in Delaware has been a blessing. The overflow is abundant in Delaware, and I didn't think that could happen. My family has grown closer, I am a licensed minister at a local church, I thrive in my workplace, and I have the opportunity to reach so many people within the community.

I have the opportunity to watch my little sister grow up and attend her volleyball games. I enjoy the comfort of sitting in my mom's office and listening to her advice. I am here and present. I am thankful for my supportive family. We have our quirks and issues, but I know they have my back. I wish I would've realized this sooner rather than later. Trust me, I still have my moments. Being independent yet living closer to home can be overwhelming because of the demands on my time. As much as I love my family, I value my space, and they respect the boundaries. However, I am truly grateful for every moment we get to share!

Being Present Is a Present

In this season of my life, being present means more to me than ever. Have you ever read Gary Chapman's book, The Five Love Languages? If you haven't, I'd recommend reading it soon. While reading this book, I discovered my love language is quality time. I'm the type of person who gets frustrated at the dinner table because everyone is on their cell phone. There are 22 other hours in the day to scroll, swipe, like, or comment, so please don't do it my presence. I hate it. To be present, you have to be involved, not merely taking up space.

Bless Them Anyway

Have you ever had someone who tried to get under your skin? When this happens to me, I have to remind myself that the enemy uses others to distract me from my purpose. You can see for yourself in that the enemy tries to kill, steal, and destroy. This means there is an existence of life worth killing, an establishment worthy of stealing, and a foundation and development worth destroying. Notice how I wrote "trying"; the enemy will not be able to do any of these things if you close those access points. Because we have the same power and authority that raised Jesus from the dead, we can walk with our heads held high and know that we are protected by our Great Protector. Can you imagine? Every knee shall bow and every tongue must confess that Jesus is Lord (Phil. 2:10–11)! So armor up, stand tall, and bless them anyway.

> *"Too often we run away from the storms*
> *that were intended for our growth."*

I pray I will drop down to my knees before I develop an attitude. I pray he will change me so I won't be like this world. I pray I will embrace the storms with the Holy Spirit and Jesus by my side. This is my prayer several times a day! I pray this prayer at work, in the gym, while driving, in my house, or while relaxing. Too often we run away from the storms that were intended for our growth. It's scary, yes, but thank God, he allows those storms to come so that we may learn how to trust him and have faith.

Change Even if They Don't

One night, I was studying the Word, and I started to get sleepy. I placed my Bible on my work console and prayed and asked God how he could use me. I uttered to him, "Lord, have your way with me." I brushed my teeth and walked around my work area. I know you're probably confused about my brushing my teeth at work, but it's too difficult to describe, so just go with it, okay?

My former employer's tradition was for departing employees to "tag" the wall. This tag included mementos ranging from famous quotes, sayings, and simple goodbyes. Past employees left notes on the walls—some inspirational and others not so much. As I walked around, I stumbled upon a tag that read Galatians 6:9. In my three years of working there, I had never seen that scripture on the wall before. Next to the Bible verse were the words "Jesus is Lord." Wait, two references to God in a matter of seconds? No way! I spit out my toothpaste, washed my mouth, and immediately flipped to Galatians 6:9. There, already underlined in red, it leaped off the page at me: "Let us not become weary in doing good, for at the proper time, we will reap a harvest if we do not give up." Praise God! I had asked God how I could be used by him, and his message was to keep going. You might be tired and not sure if this is the right place for you, but he has it all figured out. At the proper time, we will accomplish all the things God has in store for us, even those dreams we've kept tucked away at the back of our hearts and minds.

Even if it's been years since you last revisited a dream, why not go back to it? If you need to alter the dream, then alter it. I pray you learn from my mistakes and continue on the God-given path of your life. I see so many great things in your future. I am proud of you already!

I'll be honest. I've had a few stumbling blocks while writing this book. Those stumbling blocks include not writing the book, finding a good editor, finding a good designer, struggling with transparency, finishing the edits promptly, and so much more. However, God placed it on my heart to share my story. My message to you, friend, is that you can do it. You've made it this far, and you must continue the journey. If you want to go to college, then go. If you want your dream job, then go after it. Maintain a positive attitude, challenge yourself with new experiences, and continue to grow your faith in

God. Don't let anyone try to destroy your goals or dreams. Keep pushing, and I'll see you at the top!

Killing the Stereotypes

Can I be honest? Sometimes I use education to mask what I want to do in my adult life. I chase degrees in order not to venture into the unknown. The unknown and unfamiliar scare me. I'm nervous to try new things but love taking risks. Today, I encourage you to let go of the familiar and try something you've never done before. That's why I am finally finishing this book. That's why after this book is published, I will start my own non-profit company. I will minister to several congregations this year and have the opportunity to witness to the lost. Most importantly, I will seek God's face like never before! All of this scares me, but I'm going to do it scared.

Committed While Scared

In 2018, I committed to doing things scared. Yes, I have been blessed, and those who know me well somehow believe I am a superwoman. But honestly, my shortfalls are due to not fully committing myself. I am filled with bursts of adrenaline when starting a project but never fully commit to finishing it. I believe God gives me visions, but I don't follow through. This is not in every case of course. I have finished my master's, I have a great career, I'm blessed with a ministry, and I am a pretty decent dog mom.

Unbelieving Believer

There are other projects, however, that I've put on hold, like finishing my first book or traveling solo. Why? Because I was scared. I allowed fear to enter my heart and hinder my dreams. When I told a fellow Christian of this struggle, she told me I was an "unbelieving believer." Ouch! I was frightened by the unknown or the perception people might have of me. I believed God, but I wanted to control every area of my life. This is unbelief. God has to hold the reins of your life; you can't help him. Either you drive or he drives; we can't have it both ways.

I prayed, and God said, "DO it!" Do it scared. Do it bravely. Just do it already! I'm thankful because I'm finally finishing this book. I've also taken my first solo trip to Hong Kong. (I'm currently there now.) I work out every day except Fridays. I love working out, but I was so scared of getting too buff. I plan on living my best life...right now. Will I make mistakes? Absolutely. Do I care? Not really. Every day is a new challenge and a renewed commitment to being authentically me. Fearless and sometimes full of fear, I'm committing to doing it!

Will you commit or recommit to your dreams and goals? Even if you're scared? What's holding you back? I challenge you today to find out what is stopping you from chasing your goals. Don't delay. Where does your story begin? I hope that it starts with letting go of the familiar and trying something new. Do it today! Be intentional about your present and your future.

When I Need Him

On my best days, I need God, and on my worst days, I need him just as much. I thank him for always comforting me. It's funny I write about valuing myself and knowing my worth when the moments I beat myself up the most is when I walk with pride and lack humility. In these moments, I have taken my eyes off of God.

I didn't rely on his power and his will. I relied on my own understanding, contrary to...

Psalm 18:2 "The LORD is my rock and my fortress and my deliverer, My God, my rock, in whom I take refuge; my shield and the horn of my salvation, my stronghold."

This is my testimony, but I don't always get it right. I'm learning daily, and I have my moments I'm not proud of. It's in those moments of weakness, though, that I call on God because I'm not strong enough to survive. Thank God for His forgiveness of my faults and shortcomings. He loves me enough, and I am so thankful.

Where Am I Now?

So where am I currently? I am currently traveling solo to Hong Kong, Malaysia, and Bali. I can't believe that after months of procrastination and fear, I finally did it. It's been an adventure traveling by myself and learning more about Jasmine along this ride.

I came back from fighting for our nation's freedom a few months ago. (I deployed to the Middle East.) It's been challenging readjusting back to normalcy. I couldn't believe how scared I was to step out on faith. Being overseas changed me for the better and I am grateful for the experience.

God and others have encouraged me to document this journey of war to bless others. I'm so excited and can't wait to share it with you. My upcoming book will reveal my challenges of being deployed as a single, Christian woman. I hope it will inspire others to tackle the battle of fear and encourage them to lean on God in their worst days.

But enough about the future… Here's more about the present. I'm 29 now. God has blessed me with positions as a minister, Captain, sister, daughter, dog owner, niece, cousin, friend, leader, and follower. I recently finished my second year of seminary. God has turned my mess into a message. He's multiplied everything I've ever encountered. Every foolish and ugly thing that was meant to destroy me, He molded into a beautiful masterpiece for His glory.

God turned my homelessness into owning two homes. He turned my sinful ways into becoming an advocate for young women and men as a minister. He turned my lavish spending habits into becoming debt-free and launching a FinTech company, CreateFinStew. A creative financial stewardship company creatively designing wealth for people like you and me. He also turned my independent, "I will never get married" attitude into a healthy desire for partnership and a family. Everything the enemy used to defeat me, God worked out for my good.

> *"Friend, you are not your situation. God*
> *has a blueprint for your life."*

Friend, you are not your situation. God has a blueprint for your life. I had to be homeless to realize that I needed to stop being prideful and learn to ask for help. I lost money, but I learned the value of investing and paying back debts. I lost a couple of friends but now recognize the power of a strong network. I allowed the Holy Spirit to penetrate my heart and rid me of my cruel and evil behaviors. I allowed God to love and embrace me and continue to cling to him in my moments of fear and weakness.

I'm truly blessed and can say that God hasn't given up on me; he certainly hasn't given up on you either. I can't lie and tell you that it's been easy because there have been struggles. It's been a roller coaster ride. The transformation is remarkable, however. If only you knew! I could've been dead and gone a long time ago had it not been for the grace of God over my life.

The reality of finishing this book has led me to start new projects (that won't take seven years to finish). I am in the process of writing three more books. I am learning that as I cross off more things on my list, I am opening myself up to more time to breathe and accept new challenges from God.

Imagine a pregnant woman. She has conceived and nurtured a child for 40 weeks. But what happens if she goes over those 40 weeks, by a few months or even years? It's life-threatening because the baby requires development outside the womb. After the baby's development process, it needs to thrive without being attached to its mother. The mother must now push this baby out of her womb for the baby to survive. If we keep our dreams to ourselves, we are like an overdue pregnant woman. We need to push the idea out, no matter how messy it is. It's time to birth our goals and visions and allow God to grow and shape them.

In my experience overseas, time determines life or death. You don't have time to waste. Every minute is precious. If more people had this mindset, they would probably choose Christ earlier in life rather than waiting. They would probably go out on that blind date instead of staying home. They would probably choose to make a career change at 40.

What assignments are on your back burner? What needs to be completed so you can begin another assignment? I encourage you to keep working toward your dreams and fighting for your light. Hold onto God's unchanging hand, and watch the miracles unfold in front of your eyes. You've witnessed my story. You've heard my truth. Now it's time to speak your truth. It's time to be bold. It's time to do what God called you to do! What are you waiting for? Let's go! It's not easy, and it takes time. But it's most definitely worth it. I'm so excited for you! I can't wait to see what God does for your life and future. Thank you for reading this book. I pray you learned some truths, uncovered some deep places, allowed God to enter your heart, and, most importantly, set your truth free.

A PRAYER FOR ME

Lord, Wow. You've brought me this far. You've created in me a new heart and allowed to become the woman (or man) that I am today. I thank you for your grace, patience and willingness to see me through. You've never given up on me God and I'm so grateful. I look to you because you are my refuge, my Healer, my Deliver, my Provider. I thank you for never given up on me. I pray that I will continue to set my truth free even if it hurts (and it will hurt). I pray that I will encourage others to set their truth free. Thank you Lord for being my everything. Amen.

20-Somethings
Speaking their Truth

Katherine Lebrón | Smith College

My mother always told me, in Spanish of course, "People can take many things away from you, but they cannot take away your education." As a single mother of five who worked day and night to provide her children with children with a better life, my mother was unable to graduate from high school, let alone attend college. Seeing the struggles she faced firsthand, I dedicated my entire life to earning good grades and was eager to learn new things and experience new opportunities. I attended Fenway High School, a small "pilot" high school in Boston, MA, that taught me to work hard, be myself, and do the right thing.

Through Fenway, I was nominated for a Harvard summer program called the Crimson Summer Academy (CSA), which I attended for three consecutive summers. Through Fenway, CSA, and the Hyde Square Task Force, a community-based organization I worked for at the time, I was able to visit several colleges and universities (both in and out of state). I received more than one recommendation letter. I had my essays revised by more than one person and was guided through the college and financial aid application process. Without help from my teachers, mentors, and counselors, it would have been nearly impossible for me to navigate the college application process.

Currently, I am a dance instructor for grades K–2 at KIPP Star Elementary School in Washington Heights, New York, and I am working toward a double Master's Degree in Early Childhood Education and Special Education.

I came to KIPP through Teach for America and started as a kindergarten teacher. When our movement teacher at the time decided to leave our school, my principal approached me because she knew I was passionate about the performing arts and had experience as both a dancer and theater artist.

In this role, I use my teaching power wisely because I want all of my students to not only be successful and intelligent but also to be active agents of change in their communities. I want them to want the best for themselves and those around them.

As the proverb says, "It takes a village to raise a child." It is up to all of you to help ensure that our children are educated and feel empowered to create the change that our communities so desperately need. So go to college, graduate, and be successful in the way that best suits you, but always remember where you came from, remember how you got there, and remember to pay it forward.

Tyler Heaggans | High Point University

When I approached college applications, it was based on schools that had the academic majors that I wanted to pursue. However, when you attend college, there is a good chance that you will be pulled in another direction as you will be exposed to a variety of things or become interested in something that you can develop into a career.

For myself, I was rather nervous and lost during this process as I was only the second individual in my family to ever attend college. Fortunately, I had the desire to attend college, so I reached out to my elders within the community and counselors from the inside of the school, with whom I was comfortable expressing thoughts and concerns. Also, I was able to tour colleges that I felt could be the right fit for me. (College tours are FREE. Take as many as you want!)

I received my bachelor's degree in May 2013, and I started my career with the investment bank of Credit Suisse as an analyst. With the addition of having a resourceful network and higher education degree, I was able to transition into the real world on a good note. Networking is an important task that must be done as often as possible because, in today's society, most people are hired from an internal reference or positive recommendation. Always remember that people are paying attention to how you carry yourself in different environments, so always maintain a good reputation and high level of character at all times.

Advice: "When entering college, think of it as a clean and fresh start to take risks along with doing things out of your comfort zone. Try for simple things, from joining clubs to trying new foods to gaining real-world experience via internships or volunteer work. This will make you well rounded and more diverse. You miss 100% of the shots you don't take. Take chances and take risks. That's living life with purpose!"

Carmilya Jones | U.S. Air Force Academy

In summer 2003, I was going into my sophomore year of high school. There I sat at our household computer with an application to an aviation camp somewhere in North Carolina. My mom gave it to me knowing that I was currently in the Air Force Junior Reserve Officers' Training Corps (JROTC) at school. "But, Ma! I am terrified of flying. Why would I apply to this?" I reminded her. My mother quickly responded, "Carmilya, just fill it out. You never know what might happen." With her stern encouragement, I began filling out the aviation camp application. The application required me to answer Air Force history questions. Thankfully, with the help of the world wide web, I was able to do a simple search.

I'm not sure if *Google* was around at the time, but what I found changed my life forever. I found this small college, or military university called the United States Air Force Academy, located in Colorado Springs, CO. My first thought was, "What a beautiful and cool place." When the school year started, I quickly went to my guidance counselor's office and told her of my dream to attend the Air Force Academy. She immediately chuckled. With much embarrassment, I asked her why she would laugh. "Do you know what you are going to have to do to get into an Ivy League school like that?" she asked. "No," I replied.

From there, much work was to be done, but she enrolled me in the toughest classes my school had to offer and provided resources to external agencies that could help me fulfill my dream. Fast-forward to Spring 2006 of my senior year of high school: I received a call from my Academy Liaison Officer (ALO), which is the Air Force Academy's version of a college admission officer, telling me that I was accepted into my dream school. That night, my mother and I celebrated with hugs and a few jumps on the bed. Today, I am a Captain in the United States Air Force.

Now, could I have not been accepted to my dream school? Most definitely! Could I have not been accepted to any of the five colleges and universities that I applied to? Of course. But I was determined to make a new legacy for me and my family.

Here are the lessons I learned in the process:

1. Build a support network of people you trust to be good, reliable, and knowledgeable teammates (adults and peers alike).
2. Do not doubt your ability to succeed.
3. Write out your dreams! The more you physically see that dream, the more likely you are to work toward it.
4. Do not take NO for an answer.
5. Use your resources!
6. Approach every day with a spirit of optimism, and P.U.S.H. (Pray Until Something Happens).
7. Life is a journey. Start it off right.

Many Thanks!

God – This is your book! I am so grateful I found you. I'm so glad I stopped running from you! You mean everything to me, and I pray our bond grows deeper and stronger. Thank you for your protection and your everlasting love! Thank you for never giving up on me.

Momma J – Thanks for always being the president of my fan club. You always hear my goals and encourage me every step of the way. Thanks for letting me make mistakes, dusting me off when I fail, and pushing me to continue.

Papa-San – Dad, a lot of me is you and no one can ever take that away. Thank you for cultivating my love for books and propelling my love for writing.

Amanda – Lil sis, I pray I am as much of an inspiration to you as you are to me. I love you, and I cannot wait to see what the Lord has for you in the future.

Uncle D and family – Thanks for always being a listening ear. You are my role models, and I appreciate you. Thanks for correcting me when I am dead wrong; my pride hurts, but it's worthwhile.

AF Family – You all are like blood, and I thank you for always being there for me. I am excited about our future together.

My church family – Both MT and DE families, I love you all. Your support for me is incredible. Thank you for what you do every day. You're truly making a difference.

Lauren – Thank you for always pestering me about my book and completing it. I value our friendship more than anything! I am so blessed to have you in my life!

Carmilya – Thank you for being the rider that you are. I remember when I told you I was writing a book; you said, "Of course you are because that's what you do!" I love you, and I appreciate your heart, kindness, and realness.

Bre – Thank you for always asking about the book and reading my first draft. I am forever grateful for your entrepreneurial spirit.

Jare – I love your hustle, bro. It pushes me to do better and be better. I can't wait to see the amazing blessings God has in store for you!

Michele – Thanks for giving me a chance as a young, inexperienced college student. Thank you for hearing my heart and always spewing confidence into me!

Ashley – Thank you for the awesome sugaring experience and for motivating me to finish this book!

Dr. I – Judy, thank you for allowing me to be me and for giving me an outlet to write this book. Thank you for the encouraging words and your recommendations throughout the years!

Eric M. – Thank you for all of your help with career planning and resume building. I appreciate it.

Christina – thank you for your honesty, prayers, and support in sharing my truth. I am so grateful for our friendship and sisterhood. Thank you for helping set my truth free as CADET Paul to Dr. Paul. God Bless!

New friends – I love you all and can't wait to meet you!

Zeke – thank you for always being there. I love you and am so thankful Judy brought you into my life.

Books I Recommend

Spiritual
- *Driven by Eternity: Making Your Life Count Today & Forever* John Bevere *(I'm not going to lie I haven't finished this book, but it's really good)*
- *Don't Settle for Safe* Sara Jakes Roberts

Entrepreneurship
- *Called to Create: A Biblical Invitation to Create, Innovate, and Risk* Jordan Raynor
- *Big Idea Food: A Weekly Devotional for Entrepreneurs, Side Hustlers & Dreamers* Marlena Banks

Leadership
- *The Little Black Book of Success: Laws of Leadership for Black Women* Elaine Meryl Brown, Marsha Haygood, Rhonda Joy McLean
- *We're Going to Need More Wine* Gabrielle Union
- *The Defining Decade* Dr. Meg Jay
- *The Misadventures of Awkward Black Girl* Issa Rae
- *I'm Judging You* Luvvie Ajayi
- *Becoming* Michelle Obama

Love

- *Love: The Five Love Languages* Gary Chapman
- *The Mingling of Souls* Matt Chandler

Finances

- *The Total Money Makeover: A Proven Plan for Financial Fitness* Dave Ramsey
- *The Frugalista Files* Natalie McNeal
- *The Money Manual* Tonya Rapley

Leisure

- *Their Eyes Were Watching God* Zora Neale Hurston
- *Kindred* Octavia E. Butler

Sources

Boyington, Briana. "See 20 Years of Tuition Growth at National Universities." U.S. News & World Report. Accessed July 19, 2017. https://www. usnews.com/education/ best-colleges/paying-for-college/articles/ 2017-09-20/see-20-years-of-tuition- growth-at-national-universities.

"Maya Angelou Quotes." BrainyQuote. Accessed March 1, 2018. https://www. brainyquote.com/quotes/maya_angelou_392897.

"Performance Goal-Setting." Performance Objectives and SMART Model. Accessed March 1, 2018. http://www.dartmouth.edu/~hrs/ profldev/ performance_management/performance_objective.html.

"Why does chopping an onion make you cry?" Library of Congress Web Site. Accessed October 7, 2017. https://www.loc.gov/rr/scitech/ mysteries/onion.html.

About The Author

Jasmine Paul is the founder of CreateFinStew LLC, a Fin-Tech startup transforming finances creatively. After paying off her debt in 2014, she started helping her friends and built a system to encourage financial lifestyle changes. She's served over 38 clients and encouraged the elimination of $188K in student loan/credit card debt. Jasmine is also the host of the Find & Sustain Podcast, where her listeners find truth while sustaining purpose.

Jasmine is a licensed minister and a Doctor of Ministry Student, has a Master of Science from Oklahoma State University and a Bachelor of Arts in Communications from High Point University. Jasmine also serves as an officer in the United States Armed Forces.

She loves life and loves helping others. She has a passion for finance, traveling, entrepreneurship, spending time with family and fellowship. When she's not ministering to the world financially or spiritually, she's playing with her dog, Zeke.

Follow Jasmine: @jasminelikepaul
or email her: info@createfinstew.com.

Share It!

#setyourtruthfree

Did you enjoy the book? If so, I would love to hear from you. Please email me at info@createfinstew.com or check out www.createfinstew.com

Support *Set Your Truth Free*:
- Share this book or a message in the book with a loved one or a stranger.
- Blast the book on your social media platforms. #setyourtruthfree
- Give an honest review on Amazon.com, Goodreads.com, or your social media.
- Follow us on IG: @Jasminelikepaul | @createfinstew | @findandsustain

This book was written out of love, pain, and confusion. Once I learned to speak my truth, I realized I wasn't alone. So many people have gone through similar situations, but they choose to keep it inside. Just like I did. Some mistakes and a few hardships later, I refuse to let things boil up inside of me. I refuse to sit back and watch my brothers and sisters around the world drown in silence. I set out to speak my truth daily.

CPSIA information can be obtained
at www.ICGtesting.com
Printed in the USA
LVHW081147260420
654457LV00005B/1613